Letters to America

A Letters to merica

CONTEMPORARY AMERICAN POETRY ON RACE

EDITED BY JIM DANIELS

 WAYNE STATE UNIVERSITY PRESS DETROIT

LIBRARY OF CONGRESS CATALOGING–IN–PUBLICATION DATA

Letters to America : contemporary American poetry on race / edited by

Jim Daniels

p.   cm.

ISBN 0–8143–2542–4 (pbk. : alk. paper)

1. American poetry—20th century.   2. United States—Race

relations—Poetry.   3. Racism—United States—Poetry.   Afro-

Americans—Poetry.   I. Daniels, Jim.

PS595.R32L47   1995

811'.54080355—dc20   95–19996

DESIGNER: S. R. TENENBAUM

CONTENTS

INTRODUCTION

> It is difficult
> to get the news from poems
> yet men die miserably every day
> for lack
> of what is found there.
>
> William Carlos Williams, from "Asphodel, That Greeny Flower"

Race has been and remains the single most compelling issue in this country. The poets represented here have had the courage to write about race with honesty and passion. Speaking from the experience of Black, Native American, Asian, Arabic, Hispanic, and white cultures, their diverse voices unite in a dialogue of poems which acknowledge and celebrate our differences while exploring America's shameful history of racial intolerance. From prisons to universities, from city streets to cocktail parties, these poets discover and explore the issues surrounding race in our society. Their poems are testimony to the constant racial tension in our daily lives, and to how it can damage us—all of us. They also testify to the strengths derived from family, history, myth, and language that are also a part of racial identity.

This anthology was assembled to help more people "get the news" about race in America. I hope that readers will be challenged by and changed by these poems, as I have been, and that they lead to more dialogue on this serious issue which continues to compel and often divide us.

While some may try to content themselves with the belief that we have solved our racial problems, one need only look at events from our recent history such as the Yusef Hawkins murder in Bensonhurst, the Vincent Chin murder in Detroit, the Rodney King beating and the subsequent riots in Los Angeles, and the many other less-publicized instances of racial injustice which fill our daily papers, and our city streets, to see that this explosive problem is with us here and now. We ignore the contemporary experience of race at considerable risk.

Many poets from minority groups inevitably turn to issues of racial difference and racial discrimination because these things are difficult if not impossible for them to ignore. Some poems document specific cases of racism, such as Cornelius Eady's "Sherbet," in which a white waitress ignores an interracial couple in a restaurant. Others deal with more positive racial interaction, as in Etheridge Knight's "A Wasp Woman Visits a Black Junkie in Prison," where two very different people make an attempt to connect:

After the seating
And the greeting, they fished for a denominator,
Common or uncommon;
And could only summon up the fact that both were human.

Regardless of their focus, poems on race are charged with the emotional intensity of writers personally engaged with their subject.

Knight's poem "For Black Poets Who Think of Suicide" points out how poets like himself feel a *responsibility* to the subject, unlike white poets, whom he chides for being self-absorbed and angst-ridden, and for ignoring social issues:

Black Poets should live—not lay
Their necks on railroad tracks (like the white boys do).
Black Poets should seek—but not search too much
In sweet dark caves, nor hunt for snipe
Down psychic trails (like the white boys do).

It is a more complicated choice for white poets to deal with race in their work. Race has often seemed like a dirty little secret among white writers, and among whites in general—an unacknowledged unpleasantry, versus an issue they are individually affected by. Fearful of being accused of racism, whites often avoid the whole subject.

The speaker in Ira Sadoff's poem "Civil Rights" admits that after heading down to Biloxi, Mississippi, for a civil rights march, "a Jewish boy with time to spare," he returned to his northern home, where "In my neighborhood private cops / patroled at night to help us sleep." Sadoff could have written a poem which focused only on the drama of his trip south, but instead he acknowledges his return to a safe, protected life. It is this kind of honest acknowledgment which makes clear what is at stake for white poets writing about this subject. June Jordan ends her poem, "What Would I Do White?" with the simple statement: "I would do nothing. / That would be enough." White poets have that choice—to do nothing. And when they do write about race, they can always return to the safe neighborhoods of other subjects. I have included white poets here who have made the choice to confront race because I believe their voices—my voice—are important to this discussion.

It is sometimes difficult for poets of any race to find the words to describe their encounters with racism. Writers are often frustrated by language when attempting to describe the subtle shades of racism, or the full horror of it. In Eady's "Sherbet," he writes:

> . . . . What poetry
> Could describe the
> perfect angle of
>
> This woman's back as
> She walks, just so,
> Mapping the room off
>
> Like the end of a
> Border dispute. . . .

Quincy Troupe seems to question the value of writing at all in "Boomerang: A Blatantly Political Poem":

> & sometimes eye wonder if it's worth the bother
> of it all, these poems eye (w)rite holding
> language percolating & shaped
> into metaphoric rage. . . .

But the poets represented here understand the value of making the attempt, of beginning to say what seems unspeakable. Racism is a product of the experience of all races—how race can blind you, protect you, strengthen you, expose you, etc. It is my belief, as reflected in the choice of poems in this anthology, that to understand and conquer racism, we must first try to articulate the experience of race for all. In Betsy Sholl's poem, "Outside the Depot," her white speaker goes south to register Black voters with a busload of volunteers. She befriends a local Black man while there. He later writes her to describe his beating after the bus left town. She ends the poem, "I didn't know how to write back." Maybe her letter back is this poem. In fact, many of these poems read like letters, letters telling our individual stories, stories we are unable or afraid to share face to face, bits and pieces of the larger, complex story of race in this country.

Acknowledging the experience of race often means not showing our best faces, admitting to parts of ourselves we might prefer to kept hidden. T. R. Hummer writes of the racism of his grandmother in "The Ideal":

> I will know till the day I die
> She was a good woman with ideas
>
> So vile it hurts me to remember,
> Not just because they were hers
> And I loved her, but because they were also
> Mine. . . .

Hummer resists the easy nostalgia which can blind us to the truth of our own histories. He has the courage to bring what is hidden to light, to unearth the racism he was exposed to as a child. Whites don't always see it, particularly in its more subtle forms, or we convince ourselves we are not seeing it. The white poet Ellen Bryant Voigt writes about this type of erasure in "At the Movie: Virginia, 1956":

> and still I never *saw* them on the street.
> It seemed a chivalric code
> laced the milk: you'd try not to look
> and they would try to be invisible.

This uneasy coexistence seems to the child in the poem simply "a chivalric code," not something imposed by racism.

The tension surrounding visibility is at the heart of the issue of assimilation. In "Fortune Cookie Blues," Amy Uyematsu writes of her desire to be seen, showing how racism can make one disappear: "But just last week two kids on bikes / circled me with "Ching Chong" insults, / and nothing I said could make them see me."

"When you look at me," Thylias Moss writes in "Lessons from a Mirror," "know that more than white is missing." Any simplifications or easy definitions are quickly dismissed by the complex poems gathered here. The struggle to maintain cultural identity in the face of forces which are trying to ignore or erase those cultures is a particularly dominant theme.

The resentment at the privileges afforded white Americans tempts some toward abandoning their cultural roots. Toi Derricotte writes in "Blackbottom" of a trip to the poor Black part of town:

> We had lost our voice in the suburbs, in Conant Gardens,
> where each brick house delineated a fence of silence;
> we had lost the right to sing in the street and damn
>   creation.
>
> We returned to wash our hands of them,
> to smell them
> whose very existence
> tore us down to the human.

Carroll Arnett/Gogisgi writes of the risk of striving for a middle ground in "Song of the Breed":

> Don't offend
> the fullbloods,
> don't offend
> the whites,
> stand there in
> the middle
> of the god-
> damned road
> and get hit.

In "The Race Question, (for one whose fame depends on keeping the Problem a problem)," Naomi Long Madgett writes about being pressured to limit herself to focusing on racial problems, and of her suspicion of those who might exploit these problems for their own fame: "I will not feed your hunger with my blood / Nor crown your nakedness / With jewels of my elegant pain."

While other races readily recognize and explore complex issues like those raised in the Madgett poem, the naive gestures by whites often betray a lack of understanding of these complexities. Robert Winner in "Segregated Railway Diner—1946," writes:

> I sat down in the colored section
> in my sixteen-year-old's gesture.
> He sat facing me in his life.
>
> A thin smile licked his lips
> and disappeared in the corners
> . . . .
> It buried me, that smile. It said
> I didn't know enough to sit with him
> in that lacerated corner.

"It buried me, that smile." That line captures the difficulty of making a gesture that means anything in the face of a problem that so often seems overwhelming. And yet, we have Winner's poem, another gesture, an attempt at something more meaningful.

While many of these poems, like Winner's, focus on tensions and bitterness, many others express solidarity and pride. They celebrate diverse cultures, celebrate the hard-fought victories for individual rights. In Michael Weaver's poem, "The Picnic, an Homage to Civil Rights," he describes the opening up of a segregated park:

> we frolicked like wealthy children on an English estate,
> as reluctant laws and bloodied heads
> tacked God's theses on wooden doors,
> guaranteed the canopy of the firmament above us.

The debts to the heroes of the civil rights movement are acknowledged in a number of poems, as well as those debts to family members who paid the price, who struggled under racism. In Quincy Troupe's "Poem for My Father," he pays homage to his father, who played baseball in the old Negro baseball leagues: "& you there, father, regal, as an african, obeah man . . . father, a harbinger, of shock waves, soon come."

Throughout this anthology, the emotional range is large: hate, bitterness, humor, despair, hope, anger, resignation, bewilderment, shock, envy, desire, love. Some poems whisper, some shout. They clash at times, and it is well they do—many were chosen for their provocative themes. It is not a goal of this anthology to be a representative *history* of how race has evolved as a subject in our poetry; that would be a task for a much larger book. It is hoped that these poems mix, but not blend, that they play off each other in a way that is also representative of the diversity of this country, that they construct a dialogue in the ongoing discussion of the experience of race. Sometimes the poets talk directly to each other, as in James Wright's poem for Etheridge Knight and Joy Harjo's poem for Audre Lorde, but they are always talking to the rest of us, to America.

W. H. Auden's poem, "September 1, 1939," the date Germany invaded Poland (this poem is referred to in Al Young's "W. H. Auden & Mantan Moreland"), originally ended with the line, "We must love one another or die." He later cut the line, suggesting perhaps it is naive to state it in such simple terms (we're going to die regardless), but how much simpler can it be stated? In terms of the ongoing racial crisis in this country, it is clear that Auden's line resonates into the next century. The human toll is staggering: how many lives have been lost? How many thwarted, psychologically damaged?

As America changes, becoming more racially and culturally diverse, our angry voices, and our loving voices, will inevitably mingle more frequently. As Francisco Alarcón writes in "Letter to America," from which this anthology takes its title:

> America
> understand
> once and for all:
>
> we are
> the insides
> of your body
>
> our faces
> reflect
> your future.

In recent years, American poetry has also become much more diverse, much more representative of the races and peoples who make up this country. Changes in our intellectual and cultural climate, and in society as a whole, have made it possible for many writers who had previously been excluded from our literature to be recognized and celebrated. Anthologies such as *After Aztlan: Latino Poets of the Nineties; The Open Boat: Poems from Asian America; Harper's Anthology of 20th Century Native American Poetry; Every Shut Eye Ain't Asleep: An Anthology of Poetry by African Americans Since 1945,* and many, many others have collected poems representing various races and cultures.

These are important additions to our literature, but we should not simply be content to isolate each other in ethnic enclaves. This anthology attempts to bring down the walls and put us all in one big room together, talking to each other with an emotional honesty characteristic of our best poetry, our best selves. Poems about race are often straightforward narratives; they speak directly, not symbolically. It seems that this subject compels an unveiled style. One particularly powerful example is Jimmy Santiago Baca's "So Mexicans Are Taking Jobs from Americans": "Mexicans are taking our jobs, they say instead. / What they really say is, let them die, / and the children too."

It's hard to hide in a poem, hard to be dishonest without being found out. Poetry pays a certain kind of attention to the world that allows it to explore beneath the surface of our daily lives. It is also, at its best, the most compressed, intense form of writing. Therefore, poetry seems the ideal form of literature to explore such a complex, controversial subject—it cuts through the safety and hypocrisy of the rhetoric we so often hear. In other words, with an anthology of poetry, you can include more voices, get more diversity and complex thinking in one place than with any other form of writing.

There were a number of ways to divide the material—theme, ethnicity, etc.—but since it is the project of this book to bring down the safe havens of definitions, I have chosen to simply alphabetize. It is hard to say that any poem is about just one thing, and, when dealing with such a complex subject like race, it becomes even more difficult and less valuable. Dividing the poems by theme might limit for readers the possibilities for these poems to play off of each other. Certainly, however, there are a number of themes running through these poems, and the subject index should serve as a guide for those interested in quickly finding poems tracing those themes. I hope, however, that grouping poems together in the index will help begin discussion rather than limit it. Poems resonate. The opportunity to listen for harmonies and dissonance is the experience offered by this kind of anthology.

This book is designed not only for the individual reader interested in this subject, but for use in a variety of classroom settings. While it is obvious that this anthology could be useful in many Cultural Studies courses, I hope it will also find its way into Introduction to Poetry courses and Creative Writing courses. I intend for this book to used as a model of fine, powerful, effective poetry writing. We have all read too many bad poems on "good subjects." These are good poems, period.

What compelled me, a white poet, to compile this anthology? I cannot introduce this book without getting personal, for when we talk of race, we are talking personal. I have included my own poem, "Time, Temperature," dedicated to James Baldwin, in which I try to come to terms with the racism in my own background. I dedicated the poem to Baldwin because the poem was written in response to a challenge he had issued many years before. When in graduate school at Bowling Green State University, I was fortunate to take a class with Baldwin. The class was entirely white. We all considered ourselves liberal, free of prejudice. I mean, after all, weren't we taking a class from *James Baldwin?* Time and time again, he challenged us to get beneath the surface of our self-serving declarations for racial equality.

In graduate school, I had my foot in a door that I hoped would open to a new world where becoming a writer was a real possibility. I thought I was leaving my background, and its dirty little secrets behind. I resisted Baldwin's call for honesty in that class, and continued to resist a serious examination of that past for many years. I was afraid of it. I was writing *around* it in my poems about growing up. Finally, it came pouring out in "Time, Temperature," the longest poem I had written—I had held back so much, it took a long poem to try and capture it all. The poem was a response to Baldwin, eight years late. I include that poem in the anthology in the hope that my voice as a poet will add something more personal to this project.

In "Time, Temperature," after watching a Black man get arrested, I admit, "Maybe his story is the story I want to tell. / But I do not know his story." In compiling this anthology, I set out to discover his story, and mine, and how they intersect with the stories of all races in this country. For those of us who do not know each other's stories, perhaps this is a place to begin. These poems are letters, not just to me, but to all of us, letters to America, letters which tell us each other's stories, letters which need to be read, thought about, and replied to.

JIM DANIELS

Letters to America

FRANCISCO ALARCÓN

LETTER TO AMERICA

pardon
the lag
in writing you

we were left
with few
letters

in your home
we were cast
as rugs

sometimes
on walls
though we

were almost
always
on floors

we served
you as
a table

a lamp
a mirror
a toy

if anything
we made
you laugh

in your kitchen
we became
another pan

even now
as a shadow
you use us

you fear us
you yell at us
you hate us

you shoot us
you mourn us
you deny us

and despite
everything
we

continue
being
us

America
understand
once and for all:

we are
the insides
of your body

our faces
reflect
your future

FAREEDAH ALLAH

LAWD, DESE COLORED CHILLUM

I get my degree
The Spring of '52
Walked all over this town.

Got a Brooks Brothers' suit
Shoes brand new
I was gonna knock the Whiteman down.

I had learned me some languages too
French I.
And French II.
Got a bad hat or two.

Finally got a job The Winter of '52

I practiced in the mirror
Knew just what to do
How to act like Charley
And speak like him too.

I left home early
In the morningtime
Proud as I could be

Whitewashed
Grinning
9-to-5
Bluecollar
Job
Me.

     A nappy-headed boy
     Some son of a mother . . .
     Said
            "HEY, BROTHER!"
Lawd, dese Chillum won't let you be
White for nothing.

CARROLL ARNETT/GOGISGI

POWWOW

Hair the color of
tobacco ash, the fair lady
anthro asked, Excuse
me please, . . . sir
(guess it beats Chief),

does that red patch
on your blanket symbolize
something?

        Yes mam,
it surely does, it
symbolizes that once
upon a time there
was a hole
in the blanket.

SONG OF THE BREED

Don't offend
the fullbloods,
don't offend
the whites,
stand there in
the middle
of the god-
damned road
and get hit.

RUSSELL ATKINS

LATE BUS (AFTER A SERIES OF HOLD-UPS)

Theft's hour—the bus
against the hark lights
affright from houses!
Two dark men board laughing
(their teeth, crooked)
and take a seat in back,
two men in jeans, jackets!

the bus blunders on, bounced
(the streets are deserted)
        —we wait
the men sit   still:
they say nothing,
yeah—their eyes (—sure,
we know what's up—)
one *feigns* awhile of sleep,
one coughs quickly as a signal
while the other holds—now!
—is it now?!
        watch their pockets,
their hands are moving,
one, as for a cigarette
and one *as if* finding
matches
      he reaches, reaches up
—falsely?—to pull the bell
cord   East 55
they leave the bus

it makes no difference:
four dark men board
        laughing

Jimmy Santiago Baca

SO MEXICANS ARE TAKING JOBS
FROM AMERICANS

O Yes? Do they come on horses
with rifles, and say,
                    Ese gringo, gimmee your job?

And do you, gringo, take off your ring,
drop your wallet into a blanket
spread over the ground, and walk away?

I hear Mexicans are taking your jobs away.
Do they sneak into town at night,
and as you're walking home with a whore,
do they mug you, a knife at your throat,
saying, I want your job?

Even on TV, an asthmatic leader
crawls turtle heavy, leaning on an assistant,
and from a nest of wrinkles on his face,
a tongue paddles through flashing waves
of lightbulbs, of cameramen, rasping
"They're taking our jobs away."

Well, I've gone about trying to find them,
asking just where the hell are these fighters.

The rifles I hear sound in the night
are white farmers shooting blacks and browns
whose ribs I see jutting out
and starving children,
I see the poor marching for a little work,
I see small white farmers selling out
to clean-suited farmers living in New York,
who've never been on a farm,
don't know the look of a hoof or the smell
of a woman's body bending all day long in fields.

I see this, and I hear only a few people
got all the money in this world, the rest
count their pennies to buy bread and butter.

Below that cool green sea of money,
millions and millions of people fight to live,
search for pearls in the darkest depths
of their dreams, hold their breath for years
trying to cross poverty to just having something.

The children are dead already. We are killing them,
that is what America should be saying;
on TV, in the streets, in offices, should be saying,
    "We aren't giving the children a chance to live."

    Mexicans are taking our jobs, they say instead.
    What they really say is, let them die,
    and the children too.

THERE ARE BLACK

There are black guards slamming cell gates
on black men,
And brown guards saying hello to brown
men
with numbers on their backs,
And white guards laughing with white cons,
and red guards, few, say nothing
to red inmates as they walk by to chow and cells.

There you have it, the little antpile . . .
convicts marching in straight lines, guards flying
on badged wings, permits to sting, to glut themselves
at the cost of secluding themselves from their people . .
Turning off their minds like watertaps
wrapped in gunnysacks that insulate the pipes
carrying the pale weak water to their hearts.

It gets bad when you see these same
guards
carrying buckets of blood out of cells,
see them puking at the smell, the people,
their own people slashing their wrists,
hanging themselves with belts from light outlets;
it gets bad to see them clean up the mess,
carry the blue cold body out under sheets,
and then retake their places in guard cages,
watching their people maul and mangle themselves,

And over this blood-rutted land,
the sun shines, the guards talk of horses and guns,
go to the store and buy new boots,
and the longer they work here the more powerful they
become,
taking on the presence of some ancient mummy,
down in the dungeons of prison, a mummy
that will not listen, but has a strange power

in this dark world, to be so utterly disgusting in ignorance,
and yet so proudly command so many men. . . .

And the convicts themselves, at the
mummy's
feet, blood-splattered leather, at this one's feet,
they become cobras sucking life out of their brothers,
they fight for rings and money and drugs,
in this pit of pain their teeth bare fangs,
to fight for what morsels they can. . . .

And the other convicts, guilty
of nothing but their born color, guilty of being innocent,
they slowly turn to dust in the nightly winds here,
flying in the wind back to their farms and cities.
From the gash in their hearts, sand flies up spraying
over houses and through trees,

look at the sand blow over this deserted
place,
you are looking at them.

PETER BLUE CLOUD

THE OLD MAN'S LAZY,

I heard the Indian Agent say,
has no pride, no get up
and go. Well, he came out
here and walked around my
place, that agent. Steps
all thru the milkweed and
curing wormwood; tells me
my place is overgrown
and should be made use
of.

The old split cedar
fence stands at many
angles, and much of it
lies on the ground like
a curving sentence of
stick writing. An old
language, too, black with
age, with different
shades of green of moss
and lichen.
      He always
says he understands us
Indians,
      and why don't
I fix the fence at least;
so I took some fine
hawk feathers fixed
to a miniature woven
shield
      and hung this
from an upright post
near the house.
          He
came by last week
and looked all around

again, eyed the feathers
for a long time.
                    He didn't
say anything, and he didn't
smile even, or look within
himself for the hawk.

Maybe sometime I'll
tell him that the fence
isn't mine to begin with,
but was put up by
the white guy who used
to live next door.
                    It was
years ago. He built a cabin,
then put up the fence. He
only looked at me once,
after his fence was up,
he nodded at me as if
to show that he knew I
was here, I guess.
                    It was
a pretty fence, enclosing
that guy, and I felt lucky
to be on the outside
of it.
          Well, that guy
dug holes all over his
place, looking for gold,
and I guess
               he never
found any. I watched
him grow old for over
twenty years, and bitter,
I could feel his anger
all over the place.

                    And
that's when I took to
leaving my place to do
a lot of visiting.
                    Then
one time I came home
and knew he was gone
for good.

My children would
always ask me why I
didn't move to town
and be closer to them.

Now, they
tell me I'm lucky to be
living way out here.
                    And
they bring their children
and come out and visit me,
and I can feel that they
want to live out here
too, but can't
for some reason, do it.

Each day
a different story is
told me by the fence,
the rain and wind and snow,
the sun and moon shadows,
this wonderful earth,
        this Creation.
I tell my grandchildren
many of these stories,
        perhaps
this too is one of them.

GWENDOLYN BROOKS

THE LOVERS OF THE POOR

arrive. The Ladies from the Ladies' Betterment
    League
Arrive in the afternoon, the late light slanting
In diluted gold bars across the boulevard brag
Of proud, seamed faces with mercy and murder hinting
Here, there, interrupting, all deep and debonair,
The pink paint on the innocence of fear;
Walk in a gingerly manner up the hall.
Cutting with knives served by their softest care,
Served by their love, so barbarously fair.
Whose mothers taught: You'd better not be cruel!
You had better not throw stones upon the wrens!
Herein they kiss and coddle and assault
Anew and dearly in the innocence
With which they baffle nature. Who are full,
Sleek, tender-clad, fit, fiftyish, a-glow, all
Sweetly abortive, hinting at fat fruit,
Judge it high time that fiftyish fingers felt
Beneath the lovelier planes of enterprise.
To resurrect. To moisten with milky chill.
To be a random hitching-post or plush.
To be, for wet eyes, random and handy hem.
    Their guild is giving money to the poor.
The worthy poor. The very very worthy
And beautiful poor. Perhaps just not too swarthy?
Perhaps just not too dirty nor too dim
Nor—passionate. In truth, what they could wish
Is—something less than derelict or dull.
Not staunch enough to stab, though, gaze for gaze!
God shield them sharply from the beggar-bold!
The noxious needy ones whose battle's bald
Nonetheless for being voiceless, hits one down.
    But it's all so bad! and entirely too much for
    them.
The stench; the urine, cabbage, and dead beans,
Dead porridges of assorted dusty grains,

The old smoke, *heavy* diapers, and, they're told,
Something called chitterlings. The darkness. Drawn
Darkness, or dirty light. The soil that stirs.
The soil that looks the soil of centuries.
And for that matter the *general* oldness. Old
Wood. Old marble. Old tile. Old old old.
Not homekind Oldness! Not Lake Forest, Glencoe.
Nothing is sturdy, nothing is majestic,
There is no quiet drama, no rubbed glaze, no
Unkillable infirmity of such
A tasteful turn as lately they have left,
Glencoe, Lake Forest, and to which their cars
Must presently restore them. When they're done
With dullards and distortions of this fistic
Patience of the poor and put-upon.

      They've never seen such a make-do-ness as
Newspaper rugs before! In this, this "flat,"
Their hostess is gathering up the oozed, the rich
Rugs of the morning (tattered! the bespattered. . . .)
Readies to spread clean rugs for afternoon.
Here is a scene for you. The Ladies look,
In horror, behind a substantial citizeness
Whose trains clank out across her swollen heart.
Who, arms akimbo, almost fills a door.
All tumbling children, quilts dragged to the floor
And tortured thereover, potato peelings, soft-
Eyed kitten, hunched-up, haggard, to-be-hurt.

      Their League is allotting largesse to the Lost.
But to put their clean, their pretty money, to put
Their money collected from delicate rose-fingers
Tipped with their hundred flawless rose-nails seems . . .

      They own Spode, Lowestoft, candelabra,
Mantels, and hostess gowns, and sunburst clocks,
Turtle soup, Chippendale, red satin "hangings,"
Aubussons and Hattie Carnegie. They Winter
In Palm Beach; cross the Water in June; attend,

When suitable, the nice Art Institute;
Buy the right books in the best bindings; saunter
On Michigan, Easter mornings, in sun or wind.
Oh Squalor! This sick four-story hulk, this fibre
With fissures everywhere! Why, what are bringings
Of loathe-love largesse? What shall peril hungers
So old old, what shall flatter the desolate?
Tin can, blocked fire escape and chitterling
And swaggering seeking youth and the puzzled wreckage
Of the middle-passage, and urine and stale shames
And, again; the porridges of the underslung
And children children children. Heavens! That
Was a rat, surely, off there, in the shadows? Long
And long-tailed? Gray? The Ladies from the Ladies'
Betterment League agree it will be better
To achieve the outer air that rights and steadies,
To hie to a house that does not holler, to ring
Bells elsetime, better presently to cater
To no more Possibilities, to get
Away. Perhaps the money can be posted.
Perhaps they two may choose another Slum!
Some serious sooty half-unhappy home!—
Where loathe-love likelier may be invested.

      Keeping their scented bodies in the center
Of the hall as they walk down the hysterical hall,
They allow their lovely skirts to graze no wall,
Are off at what they manage of a canter,
And, resuming all the clues of what they were,
Try to avoid inhaling the laden air.

CHARLES BUKOWSKI

the black poets

the black poets
young
come to my door—
"you Bukowski?"
"yeh. come in."

they sit and look around at the
destroyed room
and at
me.

they hand me their poems.
I read
them.

"no," I say and hand them
back.

"you don't like
them?"

"no."

"'roi Jones came down to see us at our
workshop . . ."

"I hate," I say,
"workshops."

". . . Leroi Jones, Ray Bradbury, lots of big
boys . . . they said this stuff was
good . . ."

"it's bad poetry, man. they are powdering your
ass."

"there's this big film-writer too. he started the whole
idea: Watts Writers' Workshop."

"ah, god, don't you *see?* they are tickling your
assholes! you should have burned the whole town
down! I'm sick of it!"

"you just don't understand
the poems . . ."

"I do, they are rhymers, full of
platitudes. you write bad
poetry."

"look muthafucka, I been on the radio, I been printed in the
L.A. Times!"

"oh?"

"well, that happened to
you?"

"no."

"o.k., muthafucka, you ain't seen the *last* of
me!"

I suppose I haven't. and it's useless to tell you that I am not
anti-black
because
somehow
that's when the whole subject becomes
sickening.

LORNA DEE CERVANTES

POEM FOR THE YOUNG WHITE MAN
WHO ASKED ME HOW I, AN INTELLIGENT,
WELL-READ PERSON COULD BELIEVE
IN THE WAR BETWEEN RACES

In my land there are no distinctions.
The barbed wire politics of oppression
have been torn down long ago. The only reminder
of past battles, lost or won, is a slight
rutting in the fertile fields.

In my land
people write poems about love,
full of nothing but contented childlike syllables.
Everyone reads Russian short stories and weeps.
There are no boundaries.
There is no hunger, no
complicated famine or greed.

I am not a revolutionary.
I don't even like political poems.
Do you think I can believe in a war between races?
I can deny it. I can forget about it
when I'm safe,
living on my own continent of harmony
and home, but I am not
there.

I believe in revolution
because everywhere the crosses are burning,
sharp-shooting goose-steppers round every corner,
there are snipers in the schools . . .
(I know you don't believe this.
You think this is nothing
but faddish exaggeration. But they
are not shooting at you.)

I'm marked by the color of my skin.
The bullets are discrete and designed to kill slowly.
They are aiming at my children.

These are facts.
Let me show you my wounds: my stumbling mind, my
"excuse me" tongue, and this
nagging preoccupation
with the feeling of not being good enough.

These bullets bury deeper than logic.
Racism is not intellectual.
I can not reason these scars away.

Outside my door
there is a real enemy
who hates me.

I am a poet
who yearns to dance on rooftops,
to whisper delicate lines about joy
and the blessings of human understanding.
I try. I go to my land, my tower of words and
bolt the door, but the typewriter doesn't fade out
the sounds of blasting and muffled outrage.
My own days bring me slaps on the face.
Every day I am deluged with reminders
that this is not
my land
and this is my land.

I do not believe in the war between races

but in this country
there is war.

DARYL NGEE CHINN

NOT TRANSLATION, NOT POETRY

—for those who felt "cheated"
at reading "The Laws" in *China Men*

Ask the old men in Chinatown,
the ones who washed and ironed in laundries,
cooked in restaurants, fished in San Francisco Bay,
laid rocks and track from California to Utah
and then down to Los Angeles.
These old men remember
that the rocks and snow in the Sierras
are softer and warmer than memories
of interrogators and officials on Angel Island
who said, "It is my duty to question your past,
to find out if you know where the stove was
back in your home in China. And it is my judgment
that this man who calls himself your brother
and these women who claim to be your wife and mother
are liars and will be sent back to China."

These men never had a wife to rub their tired shoulders
or to warm their bed. They never had children
climbing their laps or searching their pockets
for quarters or candy.
They never heard their mothers complaining
or saw them washing vegetables.
Even if they had owned all the tea in China,
they never drank tea with their brothers again.

That short chapter
in the middle of a book
about Chinese-American dreams fulfilled
has no darkness for your dreaming,
no scenery, demons, romance, epic,
only a spotlight on
laws, numbers, facts, dates,
history you and I
should have learned in the eleventh grade.

Go back and ask your teachers
about the California Congressman who used eloquence
and power in 1882 to argue and lobby for
the exclusion, from the pursuit of happiness in America,
of all Chinese laborers
        —would-be laundrymen, houseboys,
        fishermen, farmers, cigarmakers, gravediggers—
and about the Congressman who wrote the law
that kept all Chinese women
from entering the United States
from 1902 to 1946. Wasn't that when
your grandparents came to America?

Ask the white women who never asked their husbands
why they killed Chinese
in Utah, after they finished the railroad in 1865,
in Los Angeles in 1871,
in Rock Springs, Wyoming, in 1885.
Ask the kids who ran to the docks in 1886
to watch their fathers put pigtailed men
on steamboats in Humboldt Bay.

Ask Judge Kaufman of Detroit
who said in 1982
that Robert Ebens and Michael Nitz,
who killed Vincent Chin with a Louisville Slugger,
could have probation and a suspended fine
because Vincent Chin looked Japanese.

Pretend you are Caucasian and pregnant
like Christina Tien of Grand Ledge, Michigan.
It is New Year's Day, 1985.
Imagine how much warmth and softness
you feel when four men with knives
slash your car tires outside in the snow,
break your living room windows with crowbars
and say, "We want to speak with your husband
and any other Chinks in the house."

You don't understand my anger
and I am embarrassed, yet we can sit
here among the linen and silver
in this candlelit restaurant and talk
about the red snapper, the spinach fettucine
with dill and too much garlic, just
the way I like it.

If you still don't understand,
let's say that you and I
got illegally married in Maryland
—you're white, I'm not—
and let's imagine that it is Ching Ming,
that we are pulling weeds from and putting out tea
on Grandfather's grave in China.
Talk. Ask Grandfather's grave spirit to tell you
more than he told my father,
who came to America to be with his brothers.
Ask Grandfather why the only thing he said
about his stay in America was, "Don't send your sons
to Gold Mountain."

SKIN COLOR FROM THE SUN

I used to be
an admissions counselor
at Humboldt State University.

One day Penny, our secretary, told me to
pick up Line One.
I talked to this man from Palo Alto
about life in the dorms,
       the low cost of movies and rent,
       whether his daughter would need a car,
       the friendly people,
       the small classes of ten or fifteen.

When we were done, he thanked me
and asked my name. Daryl Chinn, I said.
Oh, he said, you speak very good English.
Where are you from?
I grew up in Richmond and El Cerrito, California, just
across the bay and north of where you're
calling from, I said.
Well, he said, where were you born?
Salt Lake City, I said.
Well then, where were your parents from?
My mother's from Austin, Texas, but
her brothers and sisters were born
in Washington, D.C., and Utah and—
—no, he interrupted, where
were your ancestors from?
Using the California English I had learned
from my mother and father,
from my teachers at Pullman Elementary,
Granada Junior High, and Harry Ells High,
I said, My father is from Southern China,
my voice flat and dead.
I wanted to ask him,
Where did you learn to speak English so well?

Where are you from, really
from?
        ✦

My wife and I spent a year in Florida teaching
at the University of Central Florida in Orlando.
One day, we were waiting at a stop light
near our kids' grade school. A busload
of junior high students pulled alongside.
Someone yelled out the window,
Go home Vietnamese.
        ✦

Sticks and stones will break my bones
but names can never hurt me.

Bullshit.
        ✦

I, a Chink, married this Yid broad.
Our kids are half-breeds, mulattos.
We drive Frog and Nazi cars,
play a Jap stereo with gook speakers
and flatlander turntable.
        ✦

In the high school locker room
one day just after we showered,
Lon, next to me,
said white boys smelled funny.
When I looked at him, he held his nose
and pointed silently at Jay
behind us. Later, at lunch time,
Jay said that without nigger boys
Coach wouldn't have a basketball team.

That year, just before I went to college,
Aunt Annie said, "Just remember,
since you're Chinese, they
can't tell what you are. Black people

won't think you're white. White people
won't know if you're colored.
Both might trust you. You can be
on either side. Use your race
to be whatever you want to be."

✦

Chinese are
—inscrutable, mysterious, unsmiling
—mathematical
—docile, unassertive, quiet
—all skinny, all short
—meticulous, precise
—all martial artists
—hairless, odorless
—good ping pong players
—poor English speakers
—studious
—nearsighted
—devious
—obsequious, sycophantic
—ancestor worshippers
—good cooks and laundry workers
—all engineers, doctors, or optometrists
—a model minority
—not poets
—other_____

✦

For a very long time in Europe,
Jews were forced into ghettos,
where their lives were circumscribed—
where they could live, what they could be,
who their friends could be,
where they could travel.
Some Jews found their ways out of the ghetto.
They intermarried, changed their names,
converted to Christianity,

became doctors, lawyers, royal advisors,
university scholars, and moved into
non-Jewish neighborhoods.

During the Holocaust, Adolf Hitler
convinced blond, blue-eyed women
to have babies fathered by
blond, blue-eyed men.
During the Holocaust,
if a man or woman or child
had even one grandparent who was Jewish
that person went to the ovens.

Even the children of those
blond, blue-eyed parents,
if their skin or hair or eyes
turned dark,
went to the ovens.

✦

My children come home
with questions, complaints, reports.
My son asks, Are we half-Jewish, half-Chinese?
My daughter complains, Someone
called me a China doll.

How can we tell
what part of you is Jewish or Chinese?
I ask them. Your right eye? Your left shoulder?
Your bones? The skin below your belly button?
Tell them your ancestors came from China,
that your mother is Jewish. Tell them
you are all, both.

✦

Let's go to my house,
eat some rice, some food,
talk about these words.

✦

LUCILLE CLIFTON

in white america

1   i come to read them poems

i come to read them poems,
a fancy trick i do
like juggling with balls of light.
i stand, a dark spinner,
in the grange hall,
in the library, in the
smaller conference room,
and toss and catch as if by magic,
my eyes bright, my mouth smiling,
my singed hands burning.

2   the history

1800's in this town
fourteen longhouses were destroyed
by not these people here.
not these people
burned the crops and chopped down
all the peach trees.
not these people. these people
preserve peaches, even now.

3   the tour

"this was a female school.
my mother's mother graduated
second in her class.
they were taught embroidery,
and chenille and filigree,
ladies' learning. yes,
we have a liberal history here."
smiling she pats my darky hand.

4   the hall

in this hall
dark women
scrubbed the aisles

between the pews
on their knees.
they could not rise
to worship.
in this hall
dark women
my sisters and mothers

though i speak with the tongues
of men and of angels and
have not charity . . .

in this hall
dark women,
my sisters and mothers,
i stand
and let the church say
let the church say
let the church say
AMEN.

5   the reading

i look into none of my faces
and do the best i can.
the human hair between us
stretches but does not break.
i slide myself along it and
love them, love them all.

6   it is late

it is late
in white america.
i stand
in the light of the
7-11
looking out toward
the church

and for a moment only
i feel the reverberation
of myself
in white america
a black cat
in the belfry
hanging
and
ringing.

Sam Cornish

FANNIE LOU HAMER

fannie
lou
hamer
never
heard
of
in chicago
was known for
her
big
black
mouth
in the south
fannie lou
ate
her greens
watched
her land
and wanted
to
vote

men went
to the bottom
of the river
for wanting less
but fannie
got up
went to the courthouse

big as a fist
black as the ground
underfoot

J AYNE CORTEZ

GIVE ME THE RED
ON THE BLACK OF THE BULLET
(FOR CLAUDE REECE JR.)

Bring back the life
of Claude Reece Jr.

I want the bullet from his head
to make a Benin bronze
to make an explosion of thunder
to make a cyclone

I want the 14 years of Claude Reece Jr.
shot on the 15th day of september
shot in the back of his head
shot by a police officer
shot for being black

Give me the black on the red of the bullet
i want to make a tornado
to make an earthquake
to make a fleet of stilts
for the blackness of Claude Reece Jr.
the blackness called dangerous weapon
called resisting an arrest
called nigger threat

I want the life of the blackness of Claude Reece Jr.
i want the bullet from his head
to make a protective staff for startled children
to make hooks and studs
for warrior masks

Give me the bullet with the odor
and the smoke and the skin and
the hair of Claude Reece Jr.
i want to make power
to make power
for the blackness of Claude Reece Jr.
the blackness called pent-up frustration

called unidentified negro
called nigger revolutionary

I want the life of the blackness of Claude Reece Jr.
i want the bullet from his head
to make a protective staff for startled children
to make a Benin bronze
to make an explosion of thunder
to make a cyclone
i want the bullet to bring back the blood
of Claude Reece Jr.
i want to make justice

I want to make justice for
the blackness of Claude Reece Jr.
bring back the bullet with the blood of the blackness
of Claude Reece Jr.
i want to make justice
i want to make justice for the blackness
of Claude Reece Jr.

Jim Daniels

TIME, TEMPERATURE

—for James Baldwin

1967, Detroit. My grandfather watches
tracer bullets zing past
his window. The National Guard's taken over
Lillibridge School on the corner.

 He remembers the strike at Packard
 when they promoted blacks,
 then the riots in '43,
 how the crowds gathered on Belle Isle
 just down the road, all the bloodshed
 just down the road.

On the phone with my father, he is saying *niggers*
and my father is saying *Dad* he is saying
Dad stay in the house, stay away from the window.

 My grandfather has his theories
 why they can't take the cold
 can't skate can't swim
 why they can't park their cars
 why grape's their favorite flavor
 why if you get bit by one with purple lips
 it will kill you.

My father shakes his head into thick air
saying *stay away, stay away.*
A drop of sweat hits the dirty kitchen floor.
Dad. Dad. My father's long sigh.
 ✦

Eenie, meanie miney moe
catch a nigger by the toe
our toes wedged in a tight circle
to see who'd be It. My mother
wouldn't let us say *nigger.*
She said say *froggy.*

We said *froggy*. The other kids said
froggy?

She washed my mouth with soap.
Where did you hear that word?
Everywhere. *Where?*
    ✦

1967. Eleven, I climbed on the garage
with my father's camera. In the streaked photos
flocks of helicopters blotch the sky, nothing
like birds. I held on to the rough shingles
as the spinning blades roared above me.
Helicopters spilled guardsmen
onto the armory lawn on Eight Mile Road,
the border between Detroit and Warren.

We lived on that edge. Sirens
wailed their crazy tune, no Motown Sound,
nothing we could dance to.

Fear of heights seemed more real
than what I heard on the radio, than rumors
panting on the street: *They're at Belmont.*
They're at Farwell Field.
They're crossing Eight Mile.

Getting up was easy. I needed help
getting down, my feet dangling in air,
the camera somersaulting down onto the grass.
    ✦

Eight Mile Road. Six lanes wide. The long barbed
shout, pale slab, sizzling fuse.

I didn't know a black person till I was nineteen.
I could have almost shouted from my porch.
    ✦

Nigger pile. Riding nigger.
Nigger pile on Tony. Nigger beard.

Nigger stompers. Nigger-rigged.
Nigger-lipped. Niggered up. Nigger toes.
Nigger Heaven. How far
you have to chase that nigger
to get that shirt? A fight, a fight
a nigger and a white.

Should I explain the terms, include an index
and glossary? Do we all possess
such footnotes, filed, hidden, backwards,
in code, watermarks revealed by light?

Plenty of words for hate around here.
Like Eskimos with snow, we have
our subtle distinctions.

No one can trace
all the secret white tunnels
or break the white code.
Invisible, white on white.
Squint and hope for the best.

✦

1970. Roger Edwards, our new history teacher,
gave us roles to play: KKK members,
Black Panthers. I was Huey Newton.
I said *honky* and *pig* a lot.
I wore a black beret. We dressed in black,
took toy guns to class.

I learned a little about the burning fuse—
Bobby Seale, H. Rap Brown, Stokeley Carmichael.
If this town don't come around . . .

We knew our town hadn't, and how it burned.
Huey Newton walking into our class
would have turned us all to tin soldiers,
turned us all to brittle glass.

Roger taught us what he could
till the nuns fired him.
He played records by Lightning Hopkins,
Coltrane, such strangeness we wanted to like
because he liked it. He let us swear in class
but he made us swear
not to say *nigger.*

✦

Our fathers worked with their fathers
in factories in Detroit and Warren,
brought their hate home in greasy lunch pails:
better watch out for that nigger.
That's a nigger department.
Don't help that nigger,
lazy nigger.

It spilled across the dinner tables,
through the muddy alleys,
across the concrete playgrounds,
into the schools, and we learned
our lessons well.

✦

1974. Black students
from Pershing High two miles away
visited Fitzgerald, my school.
We asked them questions
in a room crowded with teachers
who prompted us in whispers.
So foreign even those translators couldn't help.
Stilted as a high-school play.
Someone took pictures for the yearbook.

They filled our halls with a flavor
foreign and pungent. Some new kind of cooking
I wasn't sure about.
The next day in class we sat glum
while a perky teacher preached brotherhood.

We knew better. *They only brought*
the nice ones, somebody said.

✦

1975. I worked in a liquor store
where we didn't cash checks for blacks
but sold them booze and cigarettes.

A man held a gun to my head
where's your hiding place
where's your fuckin' hiding place?
I said we don't have a hiding place
he said *motherfucker, everybody*
got a hiding place
I said we took it to the bank
he said *I'm gonna kill you motherfucker*
where's your hiding place?

We stood there, his gun brushing my temple.
We looked each other in the eye: no recognition.
He grabbed money from the register,
took off down Eight Mile. I reached down
and fingered the cigarette carton
filled with checks and twenties.
The boss called the cops.
Fingerprints on a can of Colt .45
and no clues or suspects.
Colt .45, I said, *figures.*

I flipped through the mug shots:
some nigger, I said.

✦

Carl the gun collector
handed out rifles to the neighbors
in '67: *just in case just in case*
they cross Eight Mile. To protect
our families and homes, he said.
The right to bear arms.

My father did not take one.

In 1974 under the threat of busing
neighbors took pledges
put signs in their windows
I will not send my kids.
I will keep my kids home.
My mother took no sign.

The Supreme Court ruled against
cross-district busing.
Neighbors smiled archly
no thanks to you, as if my mother
was a scab in this union town.

                ✦

My grandparents both got mugged
on their street. My grandmother bent
into a sad old turtle in her chair
dazed and afraid, black circles
deep under her eyes in the house
her parents built.

We ate early when they came over
so they could be home before dark.
The golden rule: home before dark.

My grandfather would not move,
spraying his hose on the fire
in the abandoned house next door,
buying up the vacant lots around him
ten bucks a piece.

They watched their one good television
in a living room lined with three broken ones
so they won't know which one to take.

9000 vacant lots in their old neighborhood,
another 1000 homes empty, boarded up.

There's only three things
wrong with blacks, my grandfather said.
They lie, they steal, and they kill.
He did say *blacks.*

✦

My grandfather loaded up his old Ford
with stale baked goods from Sanders,
bruised fruit and vegetables, to distribute
to the poor for Father Connors, the priest
from the church across the street.
St. Rose, razed now, just another vacant lot.

He fixed bikes for the black kids
on his street. Kids. Kids
were kids, the contradictions
rattling around his head,
as if he had separate brains
for theory and practice,
separate hearts.

Old man. All things harden inside him.
No way to explain generations
of prejudice, poverty, and hunger,
bad schools and no hope, and hate,
no way to explain it.

In Detroit, it has always been a matter
of taking sides. *They*
drove us out of Detroit, he says.

✦

My old neighborhood in Warren
redlined. Too close
to Eight Mile. Blacks moving in.
Property values plunging.
Shoulda sold years ago,
a realtor said.

Old neighbors move out, refining their excuses.
Two streets over, a black family lines the curb
with boulders to keep cars off their lawn.

✦

A black guy on the assembly line
offered to break my machine for me
accidentally. I nodded.
We stood together, not smiling
just breathing and waiting

waiting and resting
resting and sighing
sighing and nodding.

The nod. It's too easy
to say *That's the kind
of cooperation we need.*
That's the kind of cooperation we need.

✦

Dogs growl. Women peek out curtains.
A black man is delivering circulars
on a hot August afternoon in 1968
surrounded by the echo of his own steps.
He is coming up our walk.
My mother opens the door, offers him iced tea.
I sit on the stoop next to him
staring, a child staring.
My mother leans against the bricks.
I can hear his throat swallowing
the cold tea. Little
is said and what is said
is said about the heat.
Thank you, he says. *Back to work.*

Hope your mom washed that glass good.
Something I will hear from time
to time. Not too loud or
too mean, but I will hear it.

◆

1980. In the department store,
those foam packing chips that last forever
poured from an overhead funnel
into gift boxes full of vases, clocks, books,
ceramic dogs, martini glasses, china, silver.
To cushion and protect.

Kim's dark skin
surrounded by the white, white foam.
We worked in that blizzard together.
We leaned across the table toward each other
in the basement under the store
where all the black people worked,
along with me and another white kid.

We felt like robots down there,
filling and sealing. Till our eyes locked
in the hard stare of mannequins.
We ate lunch together
in the lounge. People talked.
It only took me a year to ask her out.
Dixie scowled. *What are you doing?*
This is Detroit you're talking about.

We went to a movie in my part of town,
for coffee in her part.
I can't remember what we saw
because I held her hand in the dark
and we were alone there just like
two white kids, or two black kids.

All night the stares bit into us
like tiny bugs we couldn't see.
Walking to the car, I squeezed
her hand into a fist.
I guess you have to be rich

to get away with it, she said
and maybe she was right.

Our own sizzling skins could not
our own good fire could not blend
or overwhelm or distract or soothe enough.
We were not rich enough or fast enough, fat enough
or thick-and-thin enough. We could not slam
our car doors loud enough to break the long stare.

In her apartment, her child cried
upstairs while we held each other on the couch.

Go home white boy, somebody yelled
when I got in my car.

At work the next day
the foam rained down between us.
It lay in heaps.
I couldn't look at her.
I grabbed two handfuls and squeezed:
nothing can destroy them.

✦

I said *some nigger robbed the store*
and the cop said *What else is new?*
Get a gun, he said.
The board tilts, and all the balls
roll into the same hole.

I felt bad, but I said it anyway.
My shrunken head, tiny eyes
sewn shut. There is no
immunization, no shot, no cure,
no pill, no magic, no saint,
no argument, no prophet,
no potion, no confession,
no gift, no miracle, no fucking miracle.

No.

✦

Last summer, the dog next door
scared away two black kids
trying to break into my basement.

I saw them running away. A week later
the same two kids cased out a house
down the street. I stood at the door
watching, sweating, heart jumping.

I stepped out toward them. They said
You keep following us you're gonna get hurt.
I said *I'm only trying to protect my property.*
They said *Listen man, you wanna get hurt?*

No, I don't want to get hurt.
Yes, I have property now,
an old house in this mixed neighborhood.
Maybe I was afraid because they were black.
Maybe they were angry because I was white.
I tried to talk calmly but I know enough
about being stoned to know
they were stoned on something.
Everybody stoned on something—
stoned on history and hate.

Everybody got a hiding place.
          ✦
Pressed flat to the shingles
a little afraid of the height
as the helicopters pass
a little afraid of the noise and sirens
a little afraid of blacks
and rumors and everything I don't understand:
why burn, why here?
          ✦
1990. Waiting for the light at Eight Mile and I-75
I see a naked black man lunge between cars,

two cops chasing him, his feet slapping
hot cement in the silence of engines idling July heat
two cops chasing him down the road
between Detroit and Warren
between two hard places
and he is naked and soft and running
till the cops wrestle him to the ground
scraping his knees and chin.
I pass by as he lies there getting cuffed.
As he lies there.

He looks a little dazed. The cops lift him
by the cuffs and he stands, his arms
tight behind him. He looks a little stoned
a little stoned on something.
The cuffs cut into his wrists
but he barely flinches.
Even naked, he barely flinches.

Maybe his story is the story I want to tell.
But I do not know his story.

I do not know what he has done.
I am telling you everything I know.

✦

Carl took his guns back
but they are someplace.
Carl moved away
but he is someplace.

I know Carl. His nose twitches
with the gunpowder of his own hate.

They are someplace.

✦

I am trying to be naive.
It has come down to this.
Naive enough to keep from being rolled
into another bitter pill.

An open fire hydrant in hot August
after an afternoon game at Tiger Stadium.
I am walking toward my car.
A young black kid, maybe six, is dancing
in his underwear in the cool spray
he is holding his wrists up toward the sky
as if to say *take me, take me like this*
and I am so hot I join him
dancing too in cutoffs and T-shirt

and I raise my arms above my head
thinking *yes, I would like to be taken like this*
and we dance under the same sun
and there is room enough for both of us
in the spray on Rosa Parks Boulevard
in Detroit in Michigan in America saying
take me take me under one big sun
that will take us, take us all
in its own good time.

Toi Derricotte

ST. PETER CLAVER

Every town with black Catholics has a St. Peter Claver's.
My first was nursery school.
Miss Maturin made us fold our towels in a regulation square
    and nap on army cots.
No mother questioned; no child sassed.
In blue pleated skirts, pants, and white shirts,
we stood in line to use the open toilets
and conserved light by walking in darkness.
Unsmiling, mostly light-skinned, we were the children of the
    middle class, preparing to take our parents' places in a
    world that would demand we fold our hands and wait.
They said it was good for us, the bowl of soup, its
    pasty whiteness;
I learned to swallow and distrust my senses.

On holy cards St. Peter's face is olive-toned, his hair
    near kinky;
I thought he was one of us who pass between the rich and
    poor, the light and dark.
Now I read he was "a Spanish Jesuit priest who labored for
    the salvation of the African Negroes and the abolition
    of the slave trade."
I was tricked again, robbed of my patron,
and left with a debt to another white man.

THE WEAKNESS

That time my grandmother dragged me
through the perfume aisles at Saks, she held me up
by my arm, hissing, "Stand up,"
through clenched teeth, her eyes
bright as a dog's
cornered in the light.
She said it over and over,
as if she were Jesus,
and I were dead. She had been
solid as a tree,
a fur around her neck, a
light-skinned matron whose car was parked, who walked
     on swirling
marble and passed through
brass openings—in 1945.
There was not even a black
elevator operator at Saks.
The saleswoman had brought velvet
leggings to lace me in, and cooed,
as if in the service of all grandmothers.
My grandmother had smiled, but not
hungrily, not like my mother
who hated them, but wanted to please,
and they had smiled back, as if
they were wearing wooden collars.
When my legs gave out, my grandmother
dragged me up and held me like God
holds saints by the
roots of the hair. I begged her
to believe I couldn't help it. Stumbling,
her face white
with sweat, she pushed me through the crowd, rushing
away from those eyes

that saw through
her clothes, under
her skin, all the way down
to the transparent
genes confessing.

BLACKBOTTOM

When relatives came from out of town,
we would drive down to Blackbottom,
drive slowly down the congested main streets
   —Beaubien and Hastings—
trapped in the mesh of Saturday night.
Freshly escaped, black middle class,
we snickered, and were proud;
the louder the streets, the prouder.
We laughed at the bright clothes of a prostitute,
a man sitting on a curb with a bottle in his hand.
We smelled barbecue cooking in dented washtubs,
    and our mouths watered.
As much as we wanted it we couldn't take the chance.

Rhythm and blues came from the windows, the throaty
    voice of a woman lost in the bass, in the drums, in the
    dirty down and out, the grind.
"I love to see a funeral, then I know it ain't mine."
We rolled our windows down so that the waves rolled over us
    like blood.
We hoped to pass invisibly, knowing on Monday we would
    return safely to our jobs, the post office and classroom.
We wanted our sufferings to be offered up as tender meat,
and our triumphs to be belted out in raucous song.
We had lost our voice in the suburbs, in Conant Gardens,
    where each brick house delineated a fence of silence;
we had lost the right to sing in the street and damn creation.

We returned to wash our hands of them,
to smell them
whose very existence
tore us down to the human.

THE STRUGGLE

We didn't want to be white—or did we?
What did we want?
In two bedrooms, side by side,
four adults, two children.
My aunt and uncle left before light.
My father went to the factory, then the cleaners.
My mother vacuumed, ironed, cooked,
pasted war coupons. In the afternoon
she typed stencils at the metal kitchen table.
I crawled under pulling on her skirt.
What did we want?
As the furniture became modern, the carpet deep, the white
ballerina on the mantel lifted her arms like some girl near
terror;
the Degas ballerinas bowed softly in a group, a gray sensual
beauty.
What did we push ourselves out of ourselves
to do? Our hands
on the doors, cooking utensils, keys; our hands
folding the paper money, tearing the bills.

CHITRA BANERJEE DIVAKARUNI

YUBA CITY SCHOOL

From the black trunk I shake out
my one American skirt, blue serge
that smells of mothballs. Again today
Neeraj came crying from school. All week
the teacher has made him sit
in the last row, next to the fat boy
who drools and mumbles,
picks at the spotted milk-blue
skin of his face, but knows
to pinch, sudden-sharp,
when she is not looking.

The books are full of black curves,
dots like the eggs the boll-weevil lays
each monsoon in furniture-cracks
in Ludhiana. Far up in front
the teacher makes word-sounds
Neeraj does not know. They float
from her mouth-cave, he says,
in discs, each a different color.

Candy-pink for the girls
in their lace dresses, marching
shiny shoes. Silk-yellow
for the boys beside them,
crisp blond hair, hands raised
in all the right answers. Behind them
the Mexicans, whose older brothers,
he tells me, carry knives,
whose catcalls and whizzing rubber bands
clash, mid-air, with the teacher's
voice, its sharp purple edge.
For him, the words are
a muddy red, flying low and heavy,
and always the one he has learned to understand:
idiot, idiot, idiot.

I heat the iron over the stove. Outside
evening blurs the shivering
in the eucalyptus. Neeraj's shadow
disappears into the hole
he is hollowing all afternoon.
The earth, he knows, is round, and if
one can tunnel all the way through,
he will end up in Punjab,
in his grandfather's mango orchard,
his grandmother's songs lighting
on his head, the old words
glowing like summer fireflies.

In the playground, Neeraj says,
invisible hands snatch at his uncut hair,
unseen feet trip him from behind,
and when he turns, ghost laughter
all around his bleeding knees.
He bites down on his lip
to keep in the crying. They are
waiting for him to open his mouth,
so they can steal his voice.

I test the iron with little drops of water
that sizzle and die. Press down
on the wrinkled cloth. The room fills
with a smell like singed flesh.
Tomorrow in my blue skirt I will go
to see the teacher, my tongue
stiff and swollen
in my unwilling mouth, my few
English phrases. She will pluck them
from me, nail shut my lips. My son
will keep sitting in the last row
among the red words that drink his voice.

Note: The boy in the poem is a Sikh immigrant, whose religion forbids the cutting
of his hair.

Jimmie Durham

COLUMBUS DAY

In school I was taught the names
Columbus, Cortez, and Pizzaro and
A dozen other filthy murderers.
A bloodline all the way to General Miles,
Daniel Boone and General Eisenhower.

No one mentioned the names
Of even a few of the victims.
But don't you remember Chaske, whose spine
Was crushed so quickly by Mr. Pizzaro's boot?
What words did he cry into the dust?

What was the familiar name
Of that young girl who danced so gracefully
That everyone in the village sang with her—
Before Cortez' sword hacked off her arms
As she protested the burning of her sweetheart?

That young man's name was Many Deeds,
And he had been a leader of a band of fighters
Called the Redstick Hummingbirds, who slowed
The march of Cortez' army with only a few
Spears and stones which now lay still
In the mountains and remember.

Greenrock Woman was the name
Of that old lady who walked right up
And spat in Columbus' face. We
Must remember that, and remember
Laughing Otter the Taino, who tried to stop
Columbus and who was taken away as a slave.
We never saw him again.

In school I learned of heroic discoveries
Made by liars and crooks. The courage
Of millions of sweet and true people
Was not commemorated.

Let us then declare a holiday
For ourselves, and make a parade that begins
With Columbus' victims and continues
Even to our grandchildren who will be named
In their honor.
Because isn't it true that even the summer
Grass here in this land whispers those names,
And every creek has accepted the responsibility
Of singing those names? And nothing can stop
The wind from howling those names around
The corners of the school.

Why else would the birds sing
So much sweeter here than in other lands?

CORNELIUS EADY

SHERBET

The problem here is that
This isn't pretty, the
Sort of thing which

Can easily be dealt with
With words. After
All it's

A horror story to sit,
A black man with
A white wife in

The middle of a hot
Sunday afternoon at
The Jefferson Hotel in

Richmond, VA, and wait
Like a criminal for service
From a young white waitress

Who has decided that
This looks like something
She doesn't want

To be a part of. What poetry
Could describe the
perfect angle of

This woman's back as
She walks, just so,
Mapping the room off

Like the end of a
Border dispute, which
Metaphor could turn

The room more perfectly
Into a group of
Islands? And when

The manager finally
Arrives, what language
Do I use

To translate the nervous
Eye motions, the yawning
Afternoon silence, the

Prayer beneath
His simple inquiries,
The sherbet which

He then brings to the table personally,
Just to be certain
The doubt

Stays on our side
Of the fence? What do
We call the rich,

Sweet taste of
Frozen oranges in
This context? What do

We call a weight that
Doesn't fingerprint,
Won't shift

And can't explode?

THRIFT

What happens when an old black man,
Toothless and raggedy,
Walks into a bank, catches
Some young, white, middle-manager's ear
With a slurred tale of coins
Hoarded from his wife and kids
(Who would only have spent them),
Leftovers from various hits
On the numbers, plus
God knows how many
Easy deceptions.

If you were this man, what
Would you do with this true believer
Who has walked through the door
Of your bank, fired up
With what he has pulled off,
Knowing that on some non-verbal level
He has encoded you
(Or someone like you)

As kindred, that only you
(Or someone like you)
Could understand this type
Of fidelity. And somehow
He guides you to the door
And through the glass you see
The trunk of this man's car,
My father's car, its springs
Low and ripe as the apricots
Sweetening on his tree
At home. He wants to give you

The weight he has built, penny
By penny. He wants you to lift
Away what you first thought of him,
Bag by precious bag. And he wants
You to do it, now.

THE SUPREMES

We were born to be gray. We went to school,
Sat in rows, ate white bread,
Looked at the floor a lot. In the back
Of our small heads

A long scream. We did what we could,
And all we could do was
Turn on each other. How the fat kids suffered!
Not even being jolly could save them.

And then there were the anal retentives,
The terrified brown-noses, the desperately
Athletic or popular. This, of course,
Was training. At home

Our parents shook their heads and waited.
We learned of the industrial revolution,
The sectioning of the clock into pie slices.
We drank cokes and twiddled our thumbs. In the
Back of our minds

A long scream. We snapped butts in the showers,
Froze out shy girls on the dance floor,
Pin-pointed flaws like radar.
Slowly we understood: this was to be the world.

We were born insurance salesmen and secretaries,
Housewives and short order cooks,
Stock room boys and repairmen,
And it wouldn't be a bad life, they promised,
In a tone of voice that would force some of us
To reach in self-defense for wigs,
Lipstick,

Sequins.

WHY DO SO FEW BLACKS
STUDY CREATIVE WRITING?

Always the same, sweet hurt,
The understanding that settles in the eyes
Sooner or later, at the end of class,
In the silence cooling in the room.
Sooner or later it comes to this,

You stand face to face with your
Younger face and you have to answer
A student, a young woman this time,

And you're alone in the classroom
Or in your office, a day or so later,
And she has to know, if all music
Begins equal, why this poem of hers
Needed a passport, a glossary,

A disclaimer. *It was as if I were . . .*
What? Talking for the first time?
Giving yourself up? Away?
There are worlds, and there are worlds,
She reminds you. She needs to know
What's wrong with me? and you want

To crowbar or spade her hurt
To the air. You want photosynthesis
To break it down to an organic language.
You want to shake *I hear you*
Into her ear, armor her life

With permission. Really, what
Can I say? That if she chooses
To remain here the term
Neighborhood will always have
A foreign stress, that there
Will always be the moment

The small, hard details
Of your life will be made
To circle their wagons?

FALSE ARREST

What seemed to have bothered him the most, after it was
        done
And he began to re-create his story for the T.V. reporter
In front of the same park bench where he had first seen
The pair of cops that would, when he approached them
To ask directions, look him over and see

What? grab him and cuff him and whisk him to
A hospital, dope him and then let him go
The next morning, innocent, what seemed
To have broken him was the second
He realized something had

Gone wrong or too far, and all that would be left
Was the right to see the moment fall,
Taking him with it, mouth agape perhaps,
The way a trout, caught, swallows that first,
Painful cup of air,

A taut desire pulling its jaw toward
What it never dreamed it
Could taste. The cops scuffle and
Tug him towards their
Squad car, a small crowd
Gathers and hoots

And suddenly he looks dead
At the camcorder, the
Moment becomes private, as if
We were sitting with him
In a doctor's office, surrounded
By the blossoms of his
Small complaints, things

He should have paid attention
To sooner than this, a professional
But disinterested prognosis
Cutting him away.

Alfred Encarnacion

BULOSAN LISTENS TO A RECORDING OF ROBERT JOHNSON

You sing a hard blues,
black man. You too have been driven:
a tumbleweed in strong wind.
I close my eyes, your voice rolls
out of the delta, sliding
over flashy chords
that clang like railroad tracks.

Gotta keep movin'
Gotta keep movin'
Blues fallin' down like hail

One summer
I worked the *wash-lye*
section of a cannery up north,
scrubbed schools of headless fish,
breathed ammonia fumes so fierce
I almost floated off
like the arm of a friend,
chopped clean at the elbow
by a cutter's machine.

Gotta keep movin'
Gotta keep movin'
Hellhound on my trail

We are the blue men, *kaibigan*,
our pockets empty of promise.
Mississippi, California—
bad luck conspires against us,
cheap wine stings in our veins.
We reel, drunk and bitter,
under the white, legal sun.
Robert Johnson/Carlos Bulosan—
our names so different,
our song the same.

MARTÍN ESPADA

BULLY

Boston, Massachusetts, 1987

In the school auditorium,
the Theodore Roosevelt statue
is nostalgic
for the Spanish-American War,
each fist lonely for a saber
or the reins of anguish-eyed horses,
or a podium to clatter with speeches
glorying in the malaria of conquest.

But now the Roosevelt school
is pronounced *Hernández.*
Puerto Rico has invaded Roosevelt
with its army of Spanish-singing children
in the hallways,
brown children devouring
the stockpiles of the cafeteria,
children painting *Taíno* ancestors
that leap naked across murals.

Roosevelt is surrounded
by all the faces
he ever shoved in eugenic spite
and cursed as mongrels, skin of one race,
hair and cheekbones of another.

Once Marines tramped
from the newsreel of his imagination;
now children plot to spray graffiti
in parrot-brilliant colors
across the Victorian mustache
and monocle.

JORGE THE CHURCH JANITOR
FINALLY QUITS

Cambridge, Massachusetts, 1989

No one asks
where I am from,
I must be
from the country of janitors,
I have always mopped this floor.
Honduras, you are a squatter's camp
outside the city
of their understanding.

No one can speak
my name,
I host the *fiesta*
of the bathroom,
stirring the toilet
like a punchbowl.
The Spanish music of my name
is lost
when the guests complain
about toilet paper.

What they say
must be true:
I am smart,
but I have a bad attitude.

No one knows
that I quit tonight,
maybe the mop
will push on without me,
sniffing along the floor
like a crazy squid
with stringy gray tentacles.
They will call it Jorge.

CALVIN FORBES

THE POET'S SHUFFLE

They applaud at the periods and sigh
During the commas.
My poems are full of carefully wrought pauses.
I read aloud until they yawn.

Should I growl or stomp my feet—
Maybe let my wrist go limp like a snake
On the edge of the podium?
But manlike I refuse to say another word.

They think I pout, that I'm sensitive,
Similar to a worm who grows again when hurting
Most. And they whisper walking out.
Man their polite smiles can cut!

I hear them say forgive the Negro
For he knows not what to do.
For a sentimental moment, the way Bo Jangles
Used to dance, I lift my big feet

And I do the poet's shuffle.
And then like Ben Jonson I recite:
My best poem is my son
And to each Shirley Temple I will give one.

But the old ladies in the front row
Will only give me the clap.
Like cannibals well fed they sleep and burp.
And I to my wife or mistress flee.

CHARLES FORT

FOR MARTIN LUTHER KING

Black swans with wings over their eyes
move out on a simple road
and flourish in their song.
They lead a memorial search-light
into America's backyard
against the stout sheriff and water hose
and they march face to face
toward foes with their empty hands.
They push their hands
into the soil, and brush over
the ears and lips of Martin's mask.
America, does it take a stage coach
ambulance, moist engine of fear,
to call out his name?

CHRISTOPHER GILBERT

PUSHING

Me and my brother would jump off the porch
mornings for a better view of the cars
that raced around the corner up Olds Ave.,
naming the make and year; this was '58
and his voice still young enough to wait for
how I'd say the names right to the air.
Cold mornings in Lansing we'd stop the mile
to school in the high-priced grocery nearly there
and the owner, maybe a decent White man
whose heavy dark hair and far Lebanese look
had caught too many kids at his candy,
would follow us down the aisles and say,
"I know what you boys is up to, big-eyed
and such, so you better be going your way—
buy something or else you got to leave."
We'd rattle the pennies we had and go
but coming home buy some nutchews to stay
and try his nerve again, because we didn't steal
but warmed ourselves till Ray would ask me why—
till, like big brothers will, one day I guessed,
"Some things you do because you want to.
Some things you do because you can't."
In what midwest warmth there was we'd laugh,
throw some snowballs high where the sun was
breaking up the clouds.

THEORY OF CURVE

"Pitching is just an illusion. You're dealing with
a man's eyes. Make him think he's getting one
thing, and give him another, and you've got him."

—Al Jackson, pitching coach of the Boston Red Sox
(August 7, 1977)

Thrown off-center
this string of white
unwinds, cheats some 60 feet.

Then the eye wakes,
rolls down the spine called curve.

Hot patch of pale
burns its ice into kiss of wind and
fear parachuting from chest to waist.
It blurs in type the eye can't read:

a line that numbs
the spine below the belt, the last
of the colored syllables—
someone's got to put it out.

The long parade against busing
stops at Fenway Park. The concessioneer
is a spy who spits in the beer.

High in the bleacher
we cheer for Willie Horton.
He legs a big brown bat.

DIANE GLANCY

KEMO SABE

In my dream I take
the white man
slap him
til he loves me.
I tie him to the house
take his land
& buffalo.
I put other words
into his mouth
words he doesn't understand
like spoonfuls
of smashed lima beans
until his cheeks
bulge.
Chew now, dear
I say.
I flick his throat
until he swallows.
He works all day
never leaves the house.
The floors shine
the sheets are starched.
He wipes grime
from the windows
until clouds dance
across the glass.
He feeds me
when I'm hungry.
I can leave whenever
I want.
Let him struggle
for his dignity
this time
let *him* remember
my name.

THE FIRST READER
SANTEE TRAINING SCHOOL, 1873

It was insane. I thought it myself. The winter
count Sits-Down-By-Mistake drew, he said it was his
name, in the school he drew in books an antelope
with an arrow in his rump the white man screaming
we killed 3 of their men. They whacked his hands
& gave him other books to read. "This is a
sailboat. It looks nice on water. John is in
the boat. He knows how to steer." Sits said it
was especially significant to read a book on
sailing when his father prays for a bucket-full to
pour on his cornrow. He clung to my neck all day.
Worried about a ship's rigging & the waters
covering the land. There's a place where it's all
water. He knew it now. But there'd NEVER be
another flood. Remember our ancient stories? The
water we came through now trapped in our ear. He
drew water-lungs on the antelope so they could
breathe in water, made a generator that pumped the
land dry. They hit him again & taped his hands.
This is a little sailboat.
De sína watopekiyapi wata cistinna.
It looks nice on the water.
Mini akan owanyag wáste hinca.
John is in the boat.
John wata kin en yanka.
Is John afraid?
John kokipa he.
John knows how to steer the boat.
John iyupse yuza onspe.
When Sits read in his own tongue they taped it
shut in his mouth.

J OY HARJO

AUTOBIOGRAPHY

We lived next door to the bootlegger, and were lucky. The
bootlegger reigned. We were a stolen people in a stolen
land. Oklahoma meant defeat. But the sacred lands have
their own plans, seep through fingers of the alcohol
spirit. Nothing can be forgotten, only left behind.

Last week I saw the river where the hickory stood; this
homeland doesn't predict a legacy of malls and hotels.
Dreams aren't glass and steel but made from the hearts of
deer, the blazing eye of a circling panther. Translating
them was to understand the death count from Alabama, the
destruction of grandchildren, famine of stories. I didn't think
I could stand it. My father couldn't. He searched out his
death with the vengeance of a warrior who has
been the hunted. It's in our blood.

Even at two I knew we were different. Could see through the
eyes of strangers that we were trespassers in the promised
land. The Sooner State glorified the thief. Everyone and no
one was Indian. You'd best forget, claim a white star. At
three my mother told me this story:

God decided to make people. He put the first batch in the
oven, kept them in too long. They burned. These were the
black people. God put in the next batch. They were un-
cooked, not done. These were the white people. But the
next batch he cooked just right, and these were the
Indian people, just like you.

By then I was confused.
At five I was designated to string beads in kindergarten. At
seven I knew how to play chicken and win. And at fourteen I
was drinking.

I found myself in a city in the Southwest at twenty-one, when
my past came into focus. It was near midnight. We were
walking home and there he was, curled in the snow on the

sidewalk, that man from Jemez. We had all been
cheated. He hid his shame beneath a cold, downy blanket.
We hid ours in poems. We took him home, where he shiv-
ered and cried through the night like a fighting storm, then
woke in the morning, knowing nothing. Later I would see
him on the street, the same age I am now. It was my long
dark hair that cued his daughter, the chili, the songs. And I
talked to him as if he were my father, with that respect, that
hunger.

I have since outlived that man from Jemez, my father and
that ragged self I chased through precarious years. But I
carry them with me the same as this body carries the heart
as a drum. Yesterday there was rain traveling east to home.
A hummingbird spoke. She was a shining piece of invisible
memory, inside the raw cortex of songs. I knew then this
was the Muscogee season of forgiveness, time of new corn,
the spiraling dance.

ANCHORAGE

for Audre Lorde

This city is made of stone, of blood, and fish.
There are Chugatch Mountains to the east
and whale and seal to the west.
It hasn't always been this way, because glaciers
who are ice ghosts create oceans, carve earth
and shape this city here, by the sound.
They swim backwards in time.

Once a storm of boiling earth cracked open
the streets, threw open the town.
It's quiet now, but underneath the concrete
is the cooking earth,
                        and above that, air
which is another ocean, where spirits we can't see
are dancing   joking   getting full
on roasted caribou, and the praying
goes on, extends out.

Nora and I go walking down 4th Avenue
and know it is all happening.
On a park bench we see someone's Athabascan
grandmother, folded up, smelling like 200 years
of blood and piss, her eyes closed against some
unimagined darkness, where she is buried in an ache
in which nothing makes
                        sense.

We keep on breathing, walking, but softer now,
the clouds whirling in the air above us.
What can we say that would make us understand
better than we do already?
Except to speak of her home and claim her
as our own history, and know that our dreams
don't end here, two blocks away from the ocean
where our hearts still batter away at the muddy shore.

And I think of the 6th Avenue jail, of mostly Native
and Black men, where Henry told about being shot at
eight times outside a liquor store in L.A., but when
the car sped away he was surprised he was alive,
no bullet holes, man, and eight cartridges strewn
on the sidewalk
                        all around him.

Everyone laughed at the impossibility of it,
but also the truth. Because who would believe
the fantastic and terrible story of all of our survival
those who were never meant
                        to survive?

MICHAEL S. HARPER

SONG: *I WANT A WITNESS*

Blacks in frame houses
call to the helicopters,
their antlered arms
spinning; jeeps pad
these glass-studded streets;
on this hill are tanks painted gold.

Our children sing
spirituals of *Motown,*
idioms these streets suckled
on a southern road.
This scene is about power,
terror, producing
love and pain and pathology;
in an army of white dust,
blacks here to *testify,*
and *testify,* and *testify,*
and *redeem,* and *redeem,*
in black smoke coming,
as they wave their arms,
as they wave their tongues.

LINDA HOGAN

THE TRUTH IS

In my left pocket a Chickasaw hand
rests on the bone of the pelvis.
In my right pocket
a white hand. Don't worry. It's mine
and not some thief's.
It belongs to a woman who sleeps in a twin bed
even though she falls in love too easily,
and walks along with hands
in her empty pockets
even though she has put them in others
for love not money.

About the hands, I'd like to say
I am a tree, grafted branches
bearing two kinds of fruit,
apricots maybe and pit cherries.
It's not that way. The truth is
we are crowded together
and knock against each other at night.
We want amnesty.

Linda, girl, I keep telling you
this is nonsense
about who loved who
and who killed who.

Here I am, taped together
like some old civilian conservation corps
passed by from the great depression
and my pockets are empty.
It's just as well since they are masks
for the soul, and since coins and keys
both have the sharp teeth of property.

Girl, I say,
it is dangerous to be a woman of two countries.
You've got your hands in the dark
of two empty pockets. Even though

you walk and whistle like you aren't afraid
you know which pocket the enemy lives in
and you remember how to fight
so you better keep right on walking.
And you remember who killed who.
For this you want amnesty
and there's that knocking on the door
in the middle of the night.

Relax, there are other things to think about.
Shoes for instance.
Now those are the true masks of the soul.
The left shoe
and the right one with its white foot.

GARRETT KAORU HONGO

REDRESS: THINKING IT THROUGH

Redress: to receive something, get in exchange
some token, collect some claim for the loss
incurred during Evacuation and the time in Camp.
"Ten cents on the dollar" is what I've heard.
For complex reasons, our property
and our souls are devalued this way,
discounted in that manner that dishes,
farm tools, unplanted seed, silverware,
and furniture were in the frantic time
the week after soldiers and civil officers
had posted the Executive Order
sending "all persons of Japanese ancestry"
living west of 99 first to holding stations
(the horsestalls at Santa Anita, Tanforan,
Tilden, and Puyallup) and then on
to the interior by train to Camp.
Ten cents. But even that's not agreed upon.
It's only a figure our committees have suggested
to put some bargain, a denomination
upon our loss, impossible to calculate.
For what would we have back? Our dead past?
The pride our parents and grandparents lost
and never got back again? Pride is a paltry
thing, a false mantle on a mannequin,
a cloak of gaudy colors fit for parades
and costume parties on drunken Halloweens.
Or our own parades in foolish August
through the L.A. smog. Complete with grand marshall
and sceptered teenage queen with retinue
(all in ball gowns and fake ermine robes)
in a topless red Cadillac de Ville
waving long, white-gloved arms
at the dumb crowd of peanut and popcorn eaters
lined up in festive array alongside the route
down San Pedro, First and Second Streets,
past the New Hotel Otani with its plush,

glassed-in garden and foyer,
and then on by the monstrous turquoise box
and subterranean parking of L.A.P.D.—
all of this a dim *mimesis* of the most insipid
and jingoistic of 40s Americana.
Is that what we want back? Our right
to be as ceremoniously homespun
as any Hoosier at the county fair?
As any cornbelt auctioneer huckstering
some plug mare or prize sow oinking in the pen?
Perhaps so. We love the world no less,
rejoice in buffoonery and cherish
our limitations much as any Sooner
or Southern evangelist might, for we,
like them, have lived in tent cities
shaken by the wind and penetrated
by the chill frosts of harsh winters
creeping west off the high plateaus
and tundraed slopes of Heart Mountain.
Like them, we wanted a place here in this country,
contrived to settle land and build our fortunes,
keep a faith going in ourselves and in the spirit
reviving in our souls as the crops came in
and the drummers and tinkers and itinerant
country preachers began to seek us out.

Redress. Our grievances for what was lost
are nothing more than loud complaints,
the first frail and clumsy gropings
through an ossuary of emotions we have shut away
behind the barbed wire we once lived behind,
the fences we walked past in the post-war return.
Our better selves, our feeling selves, the selves
we allow full range of heart without the fear
of discipline, punishment, or the self-inflicted
codes of mangled Confucian obedience fostered
by this derangement of history, are the mounds

behind the gates and guard towers (panopticons)
of all the Camps. We walked away as shades might,
without passion or consciousness,
terrorized by our own insubstantiality,
beings lacking faith, torporous and haunted
by the sallow vision of this one outrage.

Redress. This grief that dams the telling
of our history, that maddens what feeble
articulations we have, that cries in self-pity
for consolation, must have some gesture
of recognition to have it done. Redress,
give us back the soft mantle of dignity
we came here, as you did, to claim for ourselves.

LANGSTON HUGHES

SWEET WORDS ON RACE

Sweet words that take
Their own sweet time to flower
And then so quickly wilt
Within the inner ear,
Belie the budding promise
Of their pristine hour
To wither in the
Sultry air of fear.
Sweet words so brave
When danger is not near,
I've heard
So many times before,
I'd just as leave
Not hear them
Anymore.

DINNER GUEST: ME

I know I am
The Negro Problem
Being wined and dined,
Answering the usual questions
That come to white mind
Which seeks demurely
To probe in polite way
The why and wherewithal
Of darkness U.S.A.—
Wondering how things got this way
In current democratic night,
Murmuring gently
Over *fraises du bois,*
"I'm so ashamed of being white."

The lobster is delicious,
The wine divine,
And center of attention
At the damask table, mine.
To be a Problem on
Park Avenue at eight
Is not so bad.
Solutions to the Problem,
Of course, wait.

T. R. HUMMER

THE IDEAL

CARDIFF GIANT: The world's greatest hoax: made
by a Chicago stonemason, buried on a New York
State farm and later exhumed, the "Giant" in its
time fooled hundreds of thousands and is known
in our history and legends.

—text from a postcard bought in Cooperstown, N.Y.

North: the watered-down sun
Lets the light of its long life go
Shadowy over the spine
Of the Appalachians. Everything is old.

In the Rockies you want to believe
The planet has just been born,
Ragged cliff face and pure razor
Of switchback only this second ripped

Out of God's still unrevised dream
Of a place something unknown
Called humankind might live
Once the dust settles and the kinks

Work out of the idea of garden.
But these tame, torn-down mountains
Of the Northeast hardly seem Christian,
Too wind- and water-worn

To have been created at a stroke
Ex nihilo. Don't you believe it,
I can hear my grandmother saying.
Just because it's written down

In black and white don't make it so.
She had a face, her last
Years, like a washed-out field,
Eroded soil, not stone,

But that was in the level South
And she meant newspapers, not
Scripture or Emersonian stirrings
Of the soul over Nature's alphabet.

Nature to her was a farm,
And a farm was a wasted life,
But it was by God *her* life,
And she had no sympathy

For sanctimonious sentimentality.
1961: she points
To a headline. *Look here.*
These bleeding-heart Yankees

Are ruining this whole country
With their big ideas.
That's how I remember it.
But twenty-some years later, she's become

An idea herself. Days now
I've been driving in the cold
Peculiar light of northeastern summer.
I've stood on Mt. Holyoke squinting

Through smog at the hump of Monadnoc,
Have darkened in the shadow of the façade
Of Jonathan Edwards's reconstructed
Church on Northampton's square,

Then drifted west to Cooperstown
And the Susquehanna, where I lay late
In a motel room, trying to balance
A beer and the square mass

Of the *Norton Anthology* on my chest, reading
The first words of the sermon John Winthrop
Wrote on the *Arbella* in mid-Atlantic:
God Almighty in His most holy

And wise providence, hath so disposed
Of the condition of mankind, as in all times
Some must be rich, some poor, some high
And eminent in power and dignity,

Others mean and in subjection.
He was sailing in 1630
Toward a continent he had only heard of,
to found Eden in the august name

Of the Company of Massachusetts Bay,
And of course he called his sermon
"A Model of Christian Charity."
Now, near sundown, I drive straight

Toward the sun, away
From Cooperstown's Fenimore House
Where Cooper, that well-meaning ass,
Stares white-eyed from a big Platonic bust:

Drive away from the Farmers' Museum
With its blacksmith and weaver and endless
Display of artifacts tracing
The bloodline of the plow,

All on show in a barn
As elaborate as any cathedral,
Great curved beams with their woodglow
Against walls of medieval stone

Shining in loft door shafts of light.
Driving, I know now the names
And uses of outbuildings strange
To the South as Greek ruins: round

And polygonal barns, overgrown
Dutch barns, German barns, English barns
With Victorian gingerbread at the eaves
And widow's walks perched on the roof beam,

Functionless, vestigial.
These are not barns to me
But the idea of barn, unreal
And perfect, unattainable

To any farmer I ever knew,
Any farm I grew up knowing.
This is the country they came from,
Those people who haunted my people

With the shadow of hatred thrown
A hundred years: Yankees. These
Are the farms they lived on,
These are the barns their horses

Stamped and chafed in, blowing
Steam in winter air,
High-strung and hot to draw
Sleighs through landscape paintings

Of mythological snow, or charge
Breastworks at Bull Run and Shiloh.
Yankees, my grandmother said.
What do they know about us?

Her question drifts back to me
From 1961, a year
As distant as any in history.
I can't answer. The highway snakes

Through postcard upstate New York's
Edenic farms, and I am on it, lost
Except for the abstraction of map
Fading in dusklight on the car seat.

It is a problem in pure faith.
I am eleven. My grandmother,
Who I love, is shaking the headline
In my face. *What do they know*

About who we are? Who do they think they are
To try and change how we live?
I will know till the day I die
She was a good woman with ideas

So vile it hurts me to remember,
Not just because they were hers
And I loved her, but because they were also
Mine. *Nobody a thousand miles away*

Can tell us how to run things.
Our niggers know their place.
For my grandmother and for John Winthrop
Jefferson's self-evident truths

Were unnatural, ungodly, un-American.
They had their own clear notions
Of disenfranchisement and perfection.
We believe what we believe.

I believe something about this country
Turns good people into fools.
Just outside the door
Of the Farmers' Museum's impossible

Barn, I saw a lean-to built
Above a mound of earth, and lying there
A five-ton hunk of granite
Carved in the weird shape of a man.

Absurd as it seems, the whole
Nineteenth century thought the Cardiff Giant
Was a petrified human, one of us,
But larger than life. A sign

Said somebody buried it on somebody's
Farm, and when the fieldhands plowed it up
Like a freak potato, they fell to their knees.
It lies comic now under its shelter,

Legs cracked off, testicleless
Penis lacerated. But it smiles like a bad
Caricature of Adam the first morning of the Fall.
Staring down at it, I could have sworn

It knew it had been believed in.
P.T. Barnum believed,
And his faith sold tickets,
Not just for the Cardiff Giant

But for a dozen copies of it.
One year, its castoff images
Swept the whole country.
East of this highway, the good

Liberals of Boston tend
Their pre-Revolutionary houses
And the white middle class goes marching
To Boston Common against busing.

My grandmother taught me that irony, right
For the wrong reasons, too easy.
It took the flicker of police clubs
Falling on black and white

TV news to get me started
Sorting it out years later.
Tonight I'm still sorting. I believe
Human love evolves. But I'm stuck

With all I was born with, American.
We want to be larger than something.
We want to be more than ourselves.
It is dark. I turn my headlights on.

The shadows they cast span fields.

    —for John Hales
    and Joe Battaglia

DAVID IGNATOW

FOR MEDGAR EVERS

They're afraid of me
because I remind them of the ground.
The harder they step on me
the closer I am pressed to earth,
and hard, hard they step,
growing more frightened
and vicious.

          Will I live?
They will lie in the earth
buried in me
and above them a tree will grow
for shade.

HAROLD

From the west comes Harold, with a bitter smile,
and a dry hate in his voice for micks, wops,
kikes and refugees.
                         Too bad he has to work
in a Jewish hospital, admitting Jewish people,
sick or ready to give birth. He makes sure
not to raise his head while women suffer
before him as he writes slowly his data.
Or else how could he write home to the West,
to the tall sombreros and the spittin' type
that he, the climax of a pioneering dream,
works for Jews to make his bread?
Where is the gun he ought to pull
to plug them all, then swing off at a canter
for parts unknown till things cool off,
still master of his fate and fortune,
his own?
Here he mouths blasphemous phrases,
shocking his own Baptist soul. He makes free
with farts, shoots his jibes,
orders the help around.
He laces it into the assistant director,
the biggest, bloatiest doctor of them all,
and takes his something bucks a week disdainfully
for rent, food, gas to keep a car
and six-cent stamp for home.

JUNE JORDAN

WHAT WOULD I DO WHITE?

What would I do white?
What would I do clearly full
of not exactly beans nor
pearls my nose a manicure
my eyes a picture of your wall?

I would disturb the streets by
passing by so pretty kids
on stolen petty cash would look
at me like foreign
writing in the sky

I would forget my furs on any chair.
I would ignore the doormen at the knob
the social sanskrit of my life
unwilling to disclose my cosmetology,
I would forget.

Over my wine I would acquire
I would inspire big returns to equity
the equity of capital I am
accustomed to accept

like wintertime.

I would do nothing.
That would be enough.

A POEM ABOUT INTELLIGENCE
FOR MY BROTHERS AND SISTERS

A few years back and they told me Black
means a hole where other folks
got brain/it was like the cells in the heads
of Black children was out to every hour on the hour naps
Scientists called the phenomenon the Notorious
Jensen Lapse, remember?
Anyway I was thinking
about how to devise
a test for the wise
like a Stanford-Binet
for the C.I.A.
you know?
Take Einstein
being the most the unquestionable the outstanding
the maximal mind of the century
right
And I'm struggling against this lapse leftover
from my Black childhood to fathom why
anybody should say so:
E = mc squared?
I try that on this old lady live on my block:
She sweeping away Saturday night from the stoop
and mad as can be because some absolute
jackass have left a kingsize mattress where
she have to sweep around it stains and all she
don't want to know nothing about in the first place
"Mrs. Johnson!" I say, leaning on the gate
between us: "What you think about somebody come up
with an *E* equals *M C 2?*"
"How you doin," she answer me, sideways, like she don't
want to let on she know I ain
combed my hair yet and here it is
Sunday morning but still I have the nerve
to be bothering serious work with these crazy
questions about

"*E* equals what you say again, dear?"
Then I tell her, "Well
also this same guy? I think
he was undisputed Father of the Atom Bomb!"
"That right." She mumbles or grumbles, not too politely
"And dint remember to wear socks when he put on
his shoes!" I add on (getting desperate)
at which point Mrs. Johnson take herself and her broom
a very big step down the stoop away from me
"And never did nothing for nobody in particular
lessen it was a committee
and
used to say, 'What time is it?'
and
you'd say, 'Six o'clock.'
and
he'd say, 'Day or night?'
and
and he never made nobody a cup a tea
in his whole brilliant life!"
"and
(my voice rises slightly)
and
he dint never boogie neither: never!"

"Well," say Mrs. Johnson, "Well, honey,
I do guess
that's genius for you."

Lawrence Joseph

SAND NIGGER

In the house in Detroit
in a room of shadows
when grandma reads her Arabic newspaper
it is difficult for me to follow her
word by word from right to left
and I do not understand
why she smiles about the Jews
who won't do business in Beirut
"because the Lebanese
are more Jew than Jew,"
or whether to believe her
that if I pray
to the holy card of Our Lady of Lebanon
I will share the miracle.
Lebanon is everywhere
in the house: in the kitchen
of steaming pots, leg of lamb
in the oven, plates of kousa,
hushwee rolled in cabbage,
dishes of olives, tomatoes, onions,
roasted chicken, and sweets;
at the card table in the sunroom
where grandpa teaches me
to wish the dice across the backgammon board
to the number I want;
Lebanon of mountains and sea,
of pine and almond trees,
of cedars in the service
of Solomon, Lebanon
of Babylonians, Phoenicians, Arabs, Turks
and Byzantines, of the one-eyed
monk, Saint Maron,
in whose rite I am baptized;
Lebanon of my mother
warning my father not to let
the children hear,

of my brother who hears
and from whose silence
I know there is something
I will never know; Lebanon
of grandpa giving me my first coin
secretly, secretly
holding my face in his hands,
kissing me and promising me
the whole world.
My father's vocal cords bleed;
he shouts too much
at his brother, his partner,
in the grocery store that fails.
I hide money in my drawer, I have
the talent to make myself heard.
I am admonished to learn,
never to dirty my hands
with sawdust and meat.
At dinner, a cousin
describes his niece's head
severed with bullets, in Beirut,
in civil war. "More than
an eye for an eye," he demands,
breaks down, and cries.
My uncle tells me to recognize
my duty, to use my mind,
to bargain, to succeed.
He turns the diamond ring
on his finger, asks if
I know what asbestosis is,
"the lungs become like this,"
he says, holding up a fist;
he is proud to practice
law which "distributes
money to compensate flesh."
Outside the house my practice

is not to respond to remarks
about my nose or the color of my skin.
"Sand nigger," I'm called,
and the name fits: I am
the light-skinned nigger
with black eyes and the look
difficult to figure—a look
of indifference, a look to kill—
a Levantine nigger
in the city on the strait
between the great lakes Erie and St. Clair
which has a reputation
for violence, an enthusiastically
bad-tempered sand nigger
who waves his hands, nice enough
to pass, Lebanese enough
to be against his brother,
with his brother against his cousin,
with cousin and brother
against the stranger.

LONNY KANEKO

BAILEY GATZERT: THE FIRST GRADE, 1945

Miss Riley stands above me, fading fast
beneath the porcelain light that frames her face.
Her finger, raised to God, declares each word,
each careful pencil mark must fill the void
between the faded lines. She measures us
the way she measures words like *brother, house,*
like *sister, sky* and *dog.* The way she measured
Stanley by standing him against the chalkboard.

The words are always only hers. She draws
the list and keeps the rules. The sky is bruised
but never green, a house can be magenta
and sister pink but never yellow. She matches
objects to their hues. We learn her world,
but she is never part of ours. She would
never walk down alleys, never visit
one room homes too poor to invite a guest,

or running water, a stove, or ice. She hawks
us in the class. No boy dares laugh or talk.
An easel slants its errant legs as if
to trip the unaware; we tiptoe past it.
(Three long snows, a gift from Franklin D.,
has taught us how, without apology,
to live behind barbed wire and journey home.)
We know to quiet trembling mouths and hands.

Words contain our thought. They tell just who
we really are, or camouflage the fool,
the quiet stranger who lies behind the smile.
One day, I whisper, "Benjo. . . . Benjo." I try
to tell her what I mean. "What did you say?"
Her question rocks the room and laughter sails
on wings about my ears. She checks her list.
No *benjo* there. "O-benjo!" I can't lose

control: frustration pools a cadmium stain
across the floor. Miss Riley turns, her silence

a naked finger: enemy! I've mixed
American and Japanese. She rakes
her memory—does she hear the dying cries
of boys who toppled easels, erased the sky,
then grew to manhood on the way to war?
My hand's raised to heaven. I'm here. I'm here.

RICHARD KATROVAS

SKY

On the first cool day in half a year,
an October Sunday in New Orleans,
I waken happy in my new house.
You know, sunlight, breezes, bells,
coffee, thick newspaper, all that.
When I shuffle out to walk my little dog
there's a kid, fourteen maybe,
staring down and holding his dark face
in his dark hands, on the stoop
of the abandoned house next door.
His shoes are torn and cruddy;
his filthy shirt is blooming
from his back pocket; his bony torso
is ashy black and sunken. Why do I think
in childhood he wept violently and often,
that he'll spend his adolescence
constructing alternatives to weeping,
just one of which is to sit alone
in breezy morning sunlight
and dream himself beyond the dull,
fixed circumstances of his life?
My brain is glossy with the world's news,
my heart aglow with sugar and caffeine.
all over town citizens are praying or plotting,
sleeping late or taking stock.
He looks at me and mumbles he's just resting,
which means don't worry, White Bread,
I won't smash your Ford or rape your dog
or steal your VCR, just don't worry.
Drag your silly puff around the block
and disappear. Today, this hour,
I am meant for this stoop. This air
I breathe is mine all mine, this sunlight
and sputter of tiny breezes just for me.
I'm hungry, but that's okay, for now.
For now, we are quiet in the flat regard

with which we hold each other; he drops his head
once more and I walk on, recalling hunger,
the unspeakable passions it engenders,
the ugly, useless wisdom of it.
With tainted sadness I remember such
as all the elegant systems
I've since peered upon will never steel
against the acid fact of physical despair,
but when I turn and trot my little love
back home to face the kid again, to speak
to him not like a father, but to ask
him into my house to eat, he is blocks away.

BLACK ENGLISH

How to say the distance, not the difference,
is the problem.
In her Freshman composition
Shellanda writes that most men
treat cars better than they treat women,
describes her brother rubbing
wax for hours
into red-washed steel and blinding chrome;

she is hilarious and tactful implying
the absurdity of his erotic care, and suggesting
he loves women only in his dreams.

I imagine Shellanda's brother cruising
St. Charles on a Friday night, easing
his bright machine past the homes of wealthy whites.
There is no bitterness in his face, no wonder,
only the self-satisfaction of a young man
who keeps what he owns looking nice.

Maybe at home he's one mean bastard.
But on the rich strip at night just driving
and looking around, listening to loud
music and not judging, not judging
even himself, he feels the TV
in his brain click off when the soft
white of a trolly's headlamp—
blocks away—seems a false though lovely
offering for which words will not do,

and do not matter.

CAROLYN KIZER

RACE RELATIONS

I sang in the sun
of my white oasis
as you broke stone

Then I sang and paraded
for the distant martyrs
loving the unknown

They lay still in the sun
of Sharpeville and Selma
while you broke stone

When you fled tyranny
face down in the street
signing stones with your blood

Far away I fell silent
in my white oasis
ringed with smoke and guns

Martyred in safety
I signed for lost causes
You bled on   You bled on

Now I recommence singing
in a tentative voice
loving the known

I sing in the sun
and storm of the world
to the breakers of stone

You are sentenced to life
in the guilt of freedom
in the prison of memory

Haunted by brothers
who still break stone
I am sentenced to wait

And our love-hate duet
is drowned by the drum
of the breakers of stone

      for D.B.

ETHERIDGE KNIGHT

FOR BLACK POETS WHO THINK OF SUICIDE

Black Poets should live—not leap
From steel bridges (like the white boys do).
Black Poets should live—not lay
Their necks on railroad tracks (like the white boys do).
Black Poets should seek—but not search too much
In sweet dark caves, nor hunt for snipe
Down psychic trails (like the white boys do).

For Black Poets belong to Black People. Are
The Flutes of Black Lovers. Are
The Organs of Black Sorrows. Are
The Trumpets of Black Warriors.
Let All Black Poets die as Trumpets,
And be buried in the dust of marching feet.

A WASP WOMAN VISITS
A BLACK JUNKIE IN PRISON

After explanations and regulations, he
Walked warily in.
Black hair covered his chin, subscribing to
Villainous ideal.
"This can not be real," he thought, "this is a
Classical mistake;
This is a cake baked with embarrassing icing;
Somebody's got
Likely as not, a big fat tongue in cheek!
What have I to do
With a prim and proper-blooded lady?"
Christ in deed has risen
When a Junkie in prison visits with a Wasp woman.

"Hold your stupid face, man,
Learn a little grace, man; drop a notch the sacred shield.
She might have good reason,
Like: 'I was in prison and ye visited me not,' or—some such.
So sweep clear
Anachronistic fear, fight the fog,
And use no hot words."

After the seating
And the greeting, they fished for a denominator,
Common or uncommon;
And could only summon up the fact that both were human.
"Be at ease, man!
Try to please, man!—the lady is as lost as you:
'You got children, Ma'am?' " he said aloud.

THE WARDEN SAID TO ME THE OTHER DAY

The warden said to me the other day
(innocently, I think), "Say, etheridge,
why come the black boys don't run off
like the white boys do?"
I lowered my jaw and scratched my head
and said (innocently, I think), "Well, suh,
I ain't for sure, but I reckon it's 'cause
we ain't got nowheres to run to."

DARK PROPHECY: I SING OF SHINE

And, yeah, brothers
while white / america sings about the unsink-
able molly brown
(who was hustling the titanic
when it went down)
I sing to thee of Shine
the stoker who was hip enough to flee the fucking ship
and let the white folks drown
with screams on their lips
(jumped his black ass into the dark sea, Shine did,
broke free from the straining steel).
Yeah, I sing to thee of Shine
and how the millionaire banker stood on the deck
and pulled from his pockets a million dollar check
saying Shine Shine save poor me
and I'll give you all the money a black boy needs—
how Shine looked at the money and then at the sea
and said jump in mothafucka and swim like me—
And Shine swam on—Shine swam on—
and how the banker's daughter ran naked on the deck
with her pink tits trembling and her pants roun her neck
screaming Shine Shine save poor me
and I'll give you all the pussy a black boy needs—
how Shine said now pussy is good and that's no jive
but you got to swim not fuck to stay alive—
And Shine swam on Shine swam on—

How Shine swam past a preacher afloating on a board
crying save *me* nigger Shine in the name of the Lord—
and how the preacher grabbed Shine's arm and broke his
      stroke—
how Shine pulled his shank and cut the preacher's throat—
And Shine swam on—Shine swam on—
And when the news hit shore that the titanic had sunk
Shine was up in Harlem damn near drunk

YUSEF KOMUNYAKAA

REPORT FROM THE SKULL'S DIORAMA

Dr. King's photograph
comes at me from *White Nights*
like Hoover's imagination at work,

dissolving into a scenario
at Firebase San Juan Hill:
our chopper glides in closer,
down to the platoon of black GIs
back from night patrol

with five dead. Down
into a gold whirl of leaves
dust-deviling the fire base.
A field of black trees
stakes down the morning sun.

With the chopper blades
knife-fighting the air,
yellow leaflets quiver
back to the ground, clinging to us.
These men have lost their tongues,

but the red-bordered
leaflets tell us
*VC didn't kill
Dr. Martin Luther King.*
The silence etched into their skin

is also mine. Psychological
warfare colors the napalmed hill
gold-yellow. When our gunship
flies out backwards, rising
above the men left below
to blend in with the charred
landscape, an AK-47
speaks, with the leaflets
clinging to the men & stumps,
waving to me across the years.

TU DO STREET

Music divides the evening.
I close my eyes & can see
men drawing lines in the dust.
America pushes through the membrane
of mist & smoke, & I'm a small boy
again in Bogalusa. *White Only*
signs & Hank Snow. But tonight
I walk into a place where bar girls
fade like tropical birds. When
I order a beer, the mama-san
behind the counter acts as if she
can't understand, while her eyes
skirt each white face, as Hank Williams
calls from the psychedelic jukebox.
We have played Judas where
only machine-gun fire brings us
together. Down the street
black GIs hold to their turf also.
An off-limits sign pulls me
deeper into alleys, as I look
for a softness behind these voices
wounded by their beauty & war.
Back in the bush at Dak To
& Khe Sanh, we fought
the brothers of these women
we now run to hold in our arms.
There's more than a nation
inside us, as black & white
soldiers touch the same lovers
minutes apart, tasting
each other's breath,
without knowing these rooms
run into each other like tunnels
leading to the underworld.

Audre Lorde

AFTERIMAGES

I

However the image enters
its force remains within
my eyes   rockstrewn caves
where dragonfish evolve
wild for life   relentless and acquisitive
learning to survive
where there is no food
my eyes are always hungry
and remembering
however the image enters
its force remains.

A white woman stands bereft and empty
a black boy hacked into a murderous lesson
recalled in me forever
a lurch of earth on the edge of sleep
etched into my vision
food for dragonfish   learning
to live upon whatever they must eat
the fused images beneath my pain.

II

The Pearl River floods the streets of Jackson
A Mississippi summer televised.
Trapped houses kneel like sinners in the rain
a white woman climbs from her roof into a passing boat
her fingers tarry for a moment on the chimney
now awash
tearless   no longer young   she holds
a tattered baby's blanket in her arms.
A flickering afterimage of the nightmare rain
a microphone
thrust against her
flat bewildered words

"We jest come from the bank yestiddy
borrowing money to pay the income tax
now everything's gone. I never knew
it could be so hard."

Despair weighs down her voice like Pearl River mud
caked around the edges
"Hard, but not this hard."

Two towheaded children hurl themselves against her
hanging upon her coat like mirrors
and a man with hamlike hands
pulls her aside   snarls
"She ain't got nothing more to say!"

And that lie hangs in his mouth
like a shred of rotting meat.

III

I inherited Jackson, Mississippi.
For my majority it gave me Emmett Till
his 14 years puffed out like bruises
on plump boy-cheeks
his only Mississippi summer
whistling a 21-gun salute to Dixie
as a white girl passed him in the street
and he was baptized my son forever
in the midnight waters of the Pearl.

His broken body is the afterimage of my 21st year
when I walked through a northern summer
eyes averted from each corner's photography
newspapers   protest posters   magazines
Police Story   Confidential   True
the avid insistence of detail   pretending
insight or information
the length of gash across the dead boy's loins
his grieving mother's lamentation

all over
the veiled warning   the secret relish
of a Black child's mutilated body
fingered by street-corner eyes
bruise upon livid bruise.

And wherever I looked that summer
I learned to be at home with children's blood
with savored violence
with pictures of Black broken flesh
used   crumpled up   discarded
lying amid the sidewalk refuse
like a raped woman's face.

A Black boy from Chicago
whistled on the streets of Jackson, Mississippi
testing what he'd been taught
was a manly thing to do
his teachers ripped out his eyes
his sex   his tongue
and flung him to the Pearl weighted with stone
in the name of white womanhood
they took their aroused honor
back to Jackson   celebrating
in a whorehouse
the double ritual of white manhood
confirmed.

IV

*"If earth and air and water do not judge them who are we
to refuse a crust of bread?"*
Emmett Till rides the crest of the Pearl River   whistling
24 years his ghost lay like the shade of a ravished woman
and a white girl has grown older in costly honor
(what did she pay to never know its price?)
now the Pearl River speaks its muddy judgment
and I can withhold my pity and my bread.

"Hard, but not this hard."
Her face is flat with resignation and despair
with ancient and familiar sorrows
a woman surveying her crumpled future
as the white girl besmirched by Emmett's whistle
never allowed her own tongue
without power or conclusion
she stands adrift in the ruins of her honor
and a man with an executioner's face
pulls her away.

Within my eyes
flickering afterimages of a nightmare rain
a woman wrings her hands
beneath the weight of agonies remembered
I wade through summer ghosts
betrayed by visions
becoming dragonfish   surviving
the horrors we live   with
tortured lungs adapting
to breathe blood.

A woman measures her life's damage
my eyes are caves   chunks of etched rock
tied to the ghost of a Black boy
whistling   crying   frightened
her towheaded children cluster
little mirrors of despair
their father's hands already upon them
and soundlessly
a woman begins to weep.

COLLEEN J. McELROY

FOUL LINE—1987

Her back in a line straight
As an ironing board
She serves my lunch
And never shows her face
    My companion is right
    For her menu—white and male
    She gives him all her attention
    Reading his every wish
    With careful eyes as she avoids
    My gaze
Nothing personal
But all she sees is color
Black, a shadow, something dark
Near her left hip, the one she rests
Her elbow against when she wrist-
Flicks the plate dead center
On my placemat like a back-
Handed pitcher
    Such a little
    Gesture with all the effort
    Of breeding behind it
    So dainty, the proper flaunt
    Of a Southern girl's hanky
    And all within legal
If not civil limits
And I wonder vaguely if I might
Have met her in Selma
Or later opposite some other picket
Lines—we're the right age
For such encounters
    And despite laws to the contrary
    Neither of us has ever lost
    Our sense of misplacement
    And can say politely
    We both know how far we've come

FROM *HOMEGROWN: AN ASIAN-AMERICAN ANTHOLOGY OF WRITERS*

for Bee Bee Tan

I have seen this picture before
usually after a war
it is always faded brown-grey
and slightly burned around the edges
the composition is much the same
eyes full of innocence trying
vainly to guard young bodies
the boy in front is the leader
and the couple there
deliberately not holding hands
are lovers
they are all poets

they are always standing on the stairs
of some building where accordingly
they learn by generation
what lines have brought them there
the sun always washes
their various sizes with a hopeful blur
they are always the ones who want
to knit the old country to its children
and they are the ones who steal for a free
breakfast bags of oranges and cookies
for preschoolers and old ladies
who smile their appreciation

this picture holds names that are Asian
but it is much like those I've seen
on reservations or one my mother has
of me near Selma with friends
from my all-black high school
or maybe my younger brother
before his uniform was official

in this picture and the others
it is the last recognizable day

before the hills take what we know
to be our childhood
and that girl on the right will
no doubt walk a barefoot snow trail
to death and the intellect will
gain hostility with each
point of lost logic
and the writer will find
no metaphors in bullets
and their own people will
finally understand them even less
than the rest of the world

NAOMI LONG MADGETT

IMAGES

1

One student (white),
leading a class discussion
of *Native Son*
and running out of things to say,
asked, "How would you feel
if you encountered Bigger Thomas
on a dark street
late at night?"

Another student (black, astute)
countered: "How
would you know it was
Bigger Thomas?"

2

I pictured him as muscular,
dull-eyed and dense, his sullen scowl,
skin color, maze of hair
and criminal demeanor defining
my most horrendous nightmare

How can I reconcile
that image
with this tender yellow
boy who could have been
my son?

THE RACE QUESTION

(For one whose fame depends on keeping
The Problem a problem)

Would it please you if I strung my tears
In pearls for you to wear?
Would you like a gift of my hands' endless beating
Against old bars?

This time I can forget my Otherness,
Silence my drums of discontent awhile
And listen to the stars.

Wait in the shadows if you choose.
Stand alert to catch
The thunder and first sprinkle of unrest
Your insufficiency demands,
But you will find no comfort.
I will not feed your hunger with my blood
Nor crown your nakedness
With jewels of my elegant pain.

THYLIAS MOSS

LESSONS FROM A MIRROR

Snow White was nude at her wedding, she's so white
the gown seemed to disappear when she put it on.

Put me beside her and the proximity is good
for a study of chiaroscuro, not much else.

Her name aggravates me most, as if I need to be told
what's white and what isn't.

Judging strictly by appearance there's a future for me
at her heels, a shadowy protege she acknowledges only

at certain times of day. Is it fair for me to live
that way, unable to get off the ground?

Turning the tables isn't fair unless they keep turning.
Then there's the danger of Russian roulette

and my disadvantage: nothing falls from the sky
to name me.

I am empty space where the tooth was, that my tongue
rushes to fill because I can't stand vacancies.

And it's not enough. The penis just fills another
gap. And it's not enough.

When you look at me,
know that more than white is missing.

David Mura

LETTERS FROM POSTON RELOCATION CAMP (1942–45)

Dear Michiko,

Do songs sound different in prison?
I think there are more spaces between the words.
I think, when the song ends, the silence
does not stop singing. I think
there is nothing but song.

Matsuo's back, his bruises almost healed,
a tooth missing. His *biwa*
comes out again with the stars, a nightly
matter. He sends his regards.

Do you get fed these putrid gray beans?
I hope you haven't swallowed too
many of them. They put my stomach
in a permanent revolt, shouting no emperor
would ever feed his people so harshly.
I agree. Let's you and I grow
skinny together. Let's keep the peace.

Any second the lights will go off.

I look around me and see many
honest men who hide their beauty
as best they can.

I think that's what the whites hate,
our beauty, the way we carry the land
and the life of plants inside us,
seedlings and fruit, the flowers
and the flush tree, fields freed of weeds.

Why can't they see the door's inside them?
If someone found an answer to that,
they'd find an answer to why
those who are hungry and cold
go off to battle to become hungrier
and colder, farther from home.

Nine o'clock. The lights all out.

✦

Dear Michiko,

Did you hear it last night?
So many cries
clinging to the wind?

Not just the grinding
of tanks, rifles and mortars,
or the sound of eyelids
closing forever, but something
hungrier, colder.

I'm frightened. So many dying.
What do our complaints
about blankets or late letters
matter? Or even our dreams?

But this was more than a dream.

It came across seas
and the mountains,
it smelled of ash, a gasless flame,
and I woke this morning
still tired, irritable, unable to rise.

Later, bending to
the tomatoes, in line to mess,
trudging through the desert dust,
the sun plowing its furrows
on my neck, I thought

I heard them again. The cries.

I wanted to answer: my lips
were cracked, dry.

Michiko,
am I going crazy?
Did you hear them?

✦

. . . Sometimes, Michiko,
I think of my greenhouse,
how I used to stand at night in its fleshy,
steaming dark and say, "These are the most
beautiful orchids and roses in the world."
And their fragrance seeped inside me,
stayed even when I sold them.

What is it like now in Tokyo?
They say it has
sunk like a great ship.

Forgive me. Blessed
with a chance to talk to my wife,
more beautiful than any greenhouse rose,
all I can do is moan.
And yet, if I didn't tell you,
I would be angry at you for not listening,
blaming you for what I haven't spoken.

And it's too late for that . . .

When you write back, please
tell me what country I'm in.

I feel so poor now.
These words are all I own.

SHARON OLDS

ON THE SUBWAY

The young man and I face each other.
His feet are huge, in black sneakers
laced with white in a complex pattern like a
set of intentional scars. We are stuck on
opposite sides of the car, a couple of
molecules stuck in a rod of light
rapidly moving through darkness. He has
or my white eye imagines he has the
casual cold look of a mugger,
alert under hooded lids. He is wearing
red, like the inside of the body
exposed. I am wearing old fur, the
whole skin of an animal taken and
used. I look at his raw face,
he looks at my dark coat, and I don't
know if I am in his power—
he could take my coat so easily, my
briefcase, my life—
or if he is in my power, the way I am
living off his life, eating the steak
he may not be eating, as if I am taking
the food from his mouth. And he is black
and I am white, and without meaning or
trying to I must profit from his darkness,
the way he absorbs the murderous beams of the
nation's heart, as black cotton
absorbs the heat of the sun and holds it. There is
no way to know how easy this
white skin makes my life, this
life he could break so easily, the way I
think his back is being broken, the
rod of his soul that at birth was dark and
fluid, rich as the heart of a seedling
ready to thrust up into any available light.

SIMON ORTIZ

UPSTATE

Coming from Montreal
we stopped at a roadside place.
She had to use the restroom
and I stepped into the tavern.
A man, surly white drunk, told me,
"I know an Indian who dances nearby."
He wanted to show me, cursed me
because I was sullen
and didn't want to see.
She came and saved me.
I said, "It's a good thing you're white."
And she was hurt, angry.
It's an old story.
On the wall was a stuffed deerhead,
fluff falling out, blank sad eyes.
We drove madly out of the parking lot
and she didn't say anything
until we finally arrived in Vermont.

We were tired of being in the car,
our bodies and spirits cramped.
We ate in a small town.
We drove to a hillside.
The weather was muggy and hot.
I talked crummy to her, made love,
she cried, I felt sorry and bad.
I get crazy sometimes and impossible
I've heard.
          It rained hard that night.
The lights of the town below
shimmering through the rain into me.
All night long, I was lonely
and bothered by New England Indian ghosts.

DUDLEY RANDALL

BLACK POET, WHITE CRITIC

A critic advises
not to write on controversial subjects
like freedom or murder,
but to treat universal themes
and timeless symbols
like the white unicorn.

A white unicorn?

THE IDIOT

"That cop was powerful mean.
First, he called me, 'Black boy.'
Then he punched me in the face
and drug me by the collar to a wall
and made me lean against it with my hands on it
while he searched me,
and all the time he searched me
he kicked me and cuffed me and cussed me.

"I was hot enough
to lay him out,
and woulda did it, only
I didn't want to hurt his feelings,
and lose the good will
of the good white folks downtown,
who hired him."

DAVID RAY

THE ESKIMO GIRL

In Alaska an Eskimo girl
dances in a sod house,
raises her arms
as if to dance,
to show for the photograph
that she could be lifting
herself upward like flame,
happy as a courtesan.
But in the small room
of this dirt hut
her red skirt means nothing
blazing beside pain.
Hers is the honor
not of dancing
for the emperor, but of having
more radioactivity
in her blood
than any other American.
For this she has been sought
out, honored
because she ate the caribou
that stared at the horizon,
caribou which had eaten
lichen, green over the iced
rocks, lichen which had
innocently lifted into itself
the fallout of our bombs,
the magical cesium
and strontium and blue cobalt.
In a still photograph
she looks like a Thai dancer
with arms thrown out.
She looks as if she is about
to burst into flame.
Her blood is cold now,
cold by now,

it ages well on the permafrost,
it ages like the blood
of seals and caribou.
It marks the porcelain plate
of Napoleon.
But the old emperors would have let
her live, would merely have made her
one of their whores, and let her dance.

JOHN REPP

GOING FULL-COURT

Johnnie Redfern would rise above
Big Steve and dunk or fade away,
his weightless ease transfixing us
despite our need to burn him

and the other blacks we went
full-court with on Sundays
in the park our folks said
we'd never survive till the city

cleaned it up. What bodies we had
at seventeen, how true
my shot from the baseline
and what glee to hit it

over Johnnie. Strange, I recall
his lashes and thin eyebrows
most clearly. How little I knew him
or could have, though

once or twice we talked music
or maybe girls, I don't know,
but I remember wanting to say
how much I liked his moves

and the way he pissed off Big Steve
by taking all the elbows
and scoring at will, with both hands.
Basketball became the least of things

that spring, once the black kids
shut the high school down. I sat
on the heater in homeroom, watching
for my father's car, not knowing

how he'd get through the crowds,
not knowing a gang of whites

would be jumping blacks tomorrow,
or that I could open the yearbook

twenty years later and point
to the cop with his nightstick raised,
to Michelle Brown looking back at him,
her feet poised over the tar.

LEO ROMERO

IF MARILYN MONROE

If Marilyn Monroe
had been an Indian
would she have still
been considered
sexy
And would she
have become
a movie star
perhaps playing
the part
of a squaw
being raped
and massacred
over and over
in movie after movie
with many close ups
of bare breasts
and thighs
Would her hair
still have been
as golden
And would every man
in America
have wanted
to make love
to her
when their wives
weren't looking
Would she still
have made teenage
boys
grow old with longing
even if she spoke
in a tongue
no white man
could understand

and had ancestral
memories
of being driven
into a tiny corner
of America
Would America
have forgiven itself
for what it did
to this Indian
Marilyn Monroe

KATE RUSHIN

THE BLACK BACK-UPS

This is dedicated to Merry Clayton, Fontella Bass, Vonetta
Washington, Carolyn Franklin, Yolanda McCullough,
Carolyn Willis, Gwen Guthrie, Helaine Harris, and Darlene
Love. This is for all of the Black women who sang back-up
for Elvis Presley, John Denver, James Taylor, Lou Reed.
Etc. Etc. Etc.

I said Hey Babe
Take a Walk on the Wild Side
I said Hey Babe
Take a Walk on the Wild Side

And the colored girls say
Do dodo do do dodododo
Do dodo do do dodododo
Do dodo do do dodododo ooooo

This is for my Great-Grandmother Esther, my Grandmother
Addie, my grandmother called Sister, my Great-Aunt
Rachel, my Aunt Hilda, my Aunt Tine, my Aunt Breda,
my Aunt Gladys, my Aunt Helen, my Aunt Ellie,
my Cousin Barbara, my Cousin Dottie and my Great-Great-
Aunt Vene.

This is dedicated to all of the Black women riding on buses
and subways back and forth to the Main Line, Haddonfield,
Cherry Hill and Chevy Chase. This is for the women who
spend their summers in Rockport, Newport, Cape Cod and
Camden, Maine. This is for the women who open those
bundles of dirty laundry sent home from those ivy-covered
campuses.

My Great-Aunt Rachel worked for the Carters
Ever since I can remember
There was *The Boy*
Whose name I never knew
And there was *The Girl*
Whose name was Jane

Great-Aunt Rachel brought Jane's dresses for me to wear
Perfectly Good Clothes
And I should've been glad to get them
Perfectly Good Clothes
No matter they didn't fit quite right
Perfectly Good Clothes
Brought home in a brown paper bag
With an air of accomplishment and excitement
Perfectly Good Clothes
Which I hated

At school
In Ohio
I swear to Gawd
There was always somebody
Telling me that the only person
In their whole house
Who listened and understood them
Despite the money and the lessons
Was the housekeeper
And I knew it was true
But what was I supposed to say

I know it's true
I watch her getting off the train
Moving slowly toward the Country Squire
With their uniform in her shopping bag
And the closer she gets to the car
The more the two little kids jump and laugh
And even the dog is about to
Turn inside out
Because they just can't wait until she gets there
Edna Edna   Wonderful Edna

But Aunt Edna to me, or Gram, or Miz Johnson, or
Sister Johnson on Sundays

And the colored girls say
Do dodo do do dodododo
Do dodo do do dodododo
Do dodo do do dodododo ooooo

This is for Hattie McDaniel, Butterfly McQueen
Ethel Waters
Sapphire
Saphronia
Ruby Begonia
Aunt Jemima
Aunt Jemima on the Pancake Box
Aunt Jemima on the Pancake Box?
AuntJemimaonthepancakebox?
Ainchamamaonthepancakebox?
Ain't chure Mama on the pancake box?

Mama Mama
Get off that box
And come home to me
And my Mama leaps off that box
She swoops down in her nurse's cape
Which she wears on Sunday
And for Wednesday night prayer meeting
And she wipes my forehead
And she fans my face
And she makes me a cup of tea
And it don't do a thing for my real pain
Except she is my mama

Mama Mommy Mammy
Mam-mee Mam-mee
I'd Walk a Mill-yon Miles
For one of your smiles

This is for the Black Back-Ups
This is for my mama and your mama

My grandma and your grandma
This is for the thousand thousand Black Back-Ups

And the colored girls say
Do   dodo   do do   dodododo
do   dodo
*   dodo*
*   do*
*   do*

IRA SADOFF

NAZIS

Thank God they're all gone
except for one or two in Clinton Maine
who come home from work
at Scott Paper or Diamond Match
to make a few crank calls
to the only Jew in New England
they can find

These make-shift students of history
whose catalogue of facts include
every Jew who gave a dollar
to elect the current governor
every Jew who'd sell this country out
to the insatiable Israeli state

I know exactly how they feel
when they say they want to smash my face

Someone's cheated them
they want to know who it is
they want to know who makes them beg
It's true Let's Be Fair
it's tough for almost everyone
I exaggerate the facts
to make a point

Just when I thought I could walk to the market
just when Jean the check-out girl
asks me how many cords of wood I chopped
and wishes me a Happy Easter
as if I've lived here all my life

Just when I can walk into the bank
and nod at the tellers who know my name
where I work who lived in my house in 1832
who know to the penny the amount
of my tiny Jewish bank account

Just when I'm sure we can all live together
and I can dine in their saltbox dining rooms
with the melancholy painting of Christ
on the wall their only consolation
just when I can borrow my neighbor's ladder
to repair one of the holes in my roof

I pick up the phone
and listen to my instructions

I see the town now from the right perspective
the gunner in the glass bubble
of his fighter plane shadowing the tiny man
with the shopping bag and pointy nose
his overcoat two sizes too large for him
skulking from one doorway to the next
trying to make his own way home

I can see he's not one of us

CIVIL RIGHTS

Biloxi, Freedom Summer, 1964

Mississippi steamed in July,
but who expected palm trees
to shade the colonials, so elegant
I could not afford to dream there?
Every day it almost rained. I slept
in railroad cars and cardboard shacks.
Black families fed me sides of pork.

The New York suburbs brought me there.
A Jewish boy with time to spare,
my guilt grew far from Mississippi.

I picketed the Dixie Country Store.
While customers turned white with spit
at the leaflet in my hand, my hand
that quivered, paper thin,
one cop in a helmet—just one cop—
bashed my fingers, turning them to claws.

I think I liked the sight of blood.
I got my dreamy night in jail,
a decent meal, a toilet and a bed.
I curled against the cooling walls
of cinder block and listened to
the ocean break the waves to mist.

Now I'm thinking of the ruts
the dirt roads cleaned by rake,
where, that July, I kicked up dust
before I rode the bus back home
to breathe the birches and the pines.
I thought my heart was wood.
In my neighborhood private cops
patroled at night to help us sleep.

BETSY SHOLL

MIDNIGHT VAPOR LIGHT BREAKDOWN

This ladies' room fluorescence will not be ignored,
this pure malicious glare guessing my age,
not even asking for money. It tells me

I'm the only white person in the club, and it's
a shame I'm so pasty and unadorned, so nearly fog
only pity can make a move this evening, a bad light

to be left in. Two dimes, no phone book, and my car
broken down. Walking out alone, I am myself a beam
in everyone's eye, calling attention to something no one

leaning against the Rainbow Lounge intended this evening.
A sort of clarity like when the sun fires factory windows and
suddenly blind, it's midnight standing outside my useless
       car,

this guy running his hand down my arm. What's happening,
       Babe?
The whole street turns its brights on us, tells him to
hot-wire something. He leans back, testing my arm

to see if it's genuine leather, while I explain whatever
comes to mind, how I read this morning that skin's
all we've got to keep us from oozing out of ourselves,

oozing like this weird light on the faces gathering around,
the sound of glass breaking, a few chuckles I can't
translate into friendly. He's got a diamond in his nose.

He can run this scene on any speed he wants, which
right now is very slow, sliding into my car, jiggling
his head a little like he's fine tuning the pedals and dials

into a jazz I didn't know they could make.
All the while he's looking at me, no smile, looking
through me to that narrow doorway beside the bar where

stairs rise unlit and steep, which I could climb, I think,
real slow. Drive you wild. Only just then the engine

kicks in, like I'm definitely not running this show.

He eases out from the wheel. A little drum roll
on the hood, and his face so close to mine he barely
whispers. Keep revving it, Babe. Then I'm gone

under the el's fractured light, the neon rainbow shorting
out behind an ambulance taking the corner on two wheels,
which I'd like to believe is a baby wanting

to be born. I'm saying, the way he looked at me—
it was summer, our clothes were thin. I could
have gone, up those stairs with him.

OUTSIDE THE DEPOT

I loved the way it felt once, practically invincible,
moving door to door, signing up people to vote, as if those
    men
idling in cars with guns at the vent windows were just there
for background effect. They were on us a whole day
before this kid pointed them out and said, "Fear's useless.
They can't beat you into somebody you don't know." It was
    just
fact to him, walking down the road. He was 16, he'd cut
    school
to be there, said he'd worry about that after we left.

We all worried the night our bus left town,
a full moon bouncing through the trees like a dot along
the words of a song. Stomachs tightened, our words
thinned to nothing when we saw the cars outside the depot,
the kids turning their perfect dark faces away from us
to slip through the crowd as if there were still time
to surround themselves with friends in some part of town
those men wouldn't go.

Who can say anything sane about these moments?
Weeks later I got the clipping and sat up in bed
thinking the trees along the road were clearer to me
than exactly what they did to his face.
I read *tire iron*, and *chains*. Some must have held,
while others pummeled and kicked.

He told me they sang. In the road they lay,
saying the good words to themselves like three men
in an empty hall hearing love songs meant for a crowd.
Half a block from the station, they had walked right into it—
the car, the drive down some dark road, blindfolded and tied,
bouncing in ruts. They had to listen to that slow vicious snarl
learned from dogs. It hurt. Then the water stilled
and still they were there, the moon lingering in rain puddles
beside their cheeks. They didn't move all night, just sang.
Even laughed, he told me. I didn't know how to write back.

DAWN

At the day camp years ago where we drove
from the projects to an outlying municipal park,
the trees were so lush, the kids didn't know
what to do with that soft filtered light,
so unlike raw sun blasting the sidewalks.
They'd glare, spin out a wisecracking jive,

or hide their faces against a trunk, gouging
the bark. One of the tough girls, 8 years old,
high octane mouth, called me *Kotex breath*
then flopped in my lap. Sweat made her dark skin
iridescent. See them birds? she asked, leaning back.
She went to the country once, on a bus, to visit

her grandfather and he had all kinds of birds,
craziest racket you ever heard. We watched a few
fuss in and out of the leaves, catching light
on their wings, light making everything its own color,
so we couldn't tell bird wing from jiggling leaf,
and I totally believed we were all connected. Only

I wasn't thinking just then about trash in the street,
or crumbling blacktop, or what it's like to climb
twelve flights in the dark through that pissy smell,
the sound of feet rushing up behind you.
That afternoon while the top branches caught
some barely translatable breeze, I couldn't answer

when all this poured out and she put it to me—
how come, how come? Instead I traced letters
on her back for her to guess, this little girl
who the next day didn't show, and when she did
wouldn't speak to me, so I don't know what
to say about the hardness she came to,

whether it was wrong or right, I just remember
her back shaking in spasms as she threw those

rocks, making the water fly up and shine a minute before it disappeared, her back which had jerked itself away from me, as if to say—You are useless, you don't know, you don't know a thing.

GARY SOTO

MEXICANS BEGIN JOGGING

At the factory I worked
In the fleck of rubber, under the press
Of an oven yellow with flame,
Until the border patrol opened
Their vans and my boss waved for us to run.
"Over the fence, Soto," he shouted,
And I shouted that I was American.
"No time for lies," he said, and pressed
A dollar in my palm, hurrying me
Through the back door.

Since I was on his time, I ran
And became the wag to a short tail of Mexicans—
Ran past the amazed crowds that lined
The street and blurred like photographs, in rain.
I ran from that industrial road to the soft
Houses where people paled at the turn of an autumn sky.
What could I do but yell *vivas*
To baseball, milkshakes, and those sociologists
Who would clock me
As I jog into the next century
On the power of a great, silly grin.

E RNESTO TREJO

THE CLOUD UNFOLDING

It starts with the picture of my grandfather,
machine gunned in his car, Packard De Luxe, 1923.
A snapshot with poor composition, slightly
out of focus, it holds the forty-three
bullets that pushed for light or air
& which now find their black spaces and obey
our eyes. His last curse will never leave
this picture, his body will never
leave that car, his blood will forever
cake on the red upholstery
(someone pulled you out of the car, someone else
unfolded a blanket over your face not knowing
that you wanted to see that cloud unfold
over the whole sky
or gather into rain & flood your eyes.
Your last curse gave way to visions of battle,
of other men, never yourself,
dying in the heat & the dust).
In El Paso my grandfather once stayed up
all night & when the sun rose he shaved the goatee,
tapped over his heart & felt the fake passport.
Later he emerged from the hotel a businessman,
like Lenin, & walked six blocks to the train station,
a black mushroom in the fog,
a piece of shit under the sky of El Paso
or Geneva, a sky that ate his shirts & sucked
his head into a chisel of anger.
Further back, in one autumn the Eiffel went up,
a symbol of itself, & every washerwoman
felt proud of her city
(But one night, in 1936, the tower would crack,
collapsing over Los Angeles, against the pavement
dressed with spit & yellow newspapers
that told the Negroes *Burn, Generation of Vipers*
& the Mexicans *Go Back Where You Came From.*
Roosevelt, the syphilitic Jew, will sell

to the Germans tomorrow at 10:15. My father
is in his kitchen, dropping ice cubes in a glass
of water, when the phone rings & a man
tells him that his bar is in flames.
When my father arrives at the bar, nine years
of good luck go up in smoke & someone tells him
it was the Negroes, your brother refused them credit.
My father nods, not knowing why, & stands
there for hours following the slow cloud from his bar
until the sun silhouettes the church two blocks away
& he thinks *that shadow is a bad omen).*
Father, for the rest of your life, in Mexico,
you never mentioned the fire
but spoke of flappers, of Roosevelt, of Chaplin
devoured by a clock on his way to work.

GAIL TREMBLAY

INDIAN SINGING IN 20TH CENTURY AMERICA

We wake; we wake the day,
the light rising in us like sun—
our breath a prayer brushing
against the feathers in our hands.
We stumble out into streets;
patterns of wires invented by strangers
are strung between eye and sky,
and we dance in two worlds,
inevitable as seasons in one,
exotic curiosities in the other
which rushes headlong down highways,
watches us from car windows, explains
us to its children in words
that no one could ever make
sense of. The image obscures
the vision, and we wonder
whether anyone will ever hear
our own names for the things
we do. Light dances in the body,
surrounds all living things—
even the stones sing
although their songs are infinitely
slower than the ones we learn
from trees. No human voice lasts
long enough to make such music sound.
Earth breath eddies between factories
and office buildings, caresses the surface
of our skin; we go to jobs, the boss
always watching the clock to see
that we're on time. He tries to shut
out magic and hopes we'll make
mistakes or disappear. We work
fast and steady and remember
each breath alters the composition
of the air. Change moves relentless,

the pattern unfolding despite their planning—
we're always there—singing round dance
songs, remembering what supports
our life—impossible to ignore.

QUINCY TROUPE

POEM FOR MY FATHER

father, it was an honor to be there, in the dugout
with you, the glory of great black men swinging their lives
as bats, at tiny white balls
burning in at unbelievable speeds, riding up & in & out
a curve breaking down wicked, like a ball falling off a table
moving away, snaking down, screwing its stitched magic
into chitling circuit air, its comma seams spinning
toward breakdown, dipping, like a hipster
bebopping a knee-dip stride, in the charlie parker forties
wrist curling, like a swan's neck
behind a slick black back
cupping an invisible ball of dreams

& you there, father, regal, as an african, obeah man
sculpted out of wood, from a sacred tree, of no name, no
        place, origin
thick branches branching down, into cherokee & someplace
        else lost
way back in africa, the sap running dry
crossing from north carolina into georgia, inside grandmother
        mary's
womb, where your mother had you in the violence of that
        red soil
ink blotter news, gone now, into blood graves
of american blues, sponging rococo
truth long gone as dinosaurs
the agent-oranged landscape of former names
absent of african polysyllables, dry husk consonants there
now, in their place, names, flat, as polluted rivers
& that guitar string smile always snaking across
some virulent, american, redneck's face
scorching, like atomic heat, mushrooming over nagasaki
& hiroshima, the fever blistered shadows of it all
inked, as etchings, into sizzled concrete

but you, there, father, through it all, a yardbird solo
riffing on bat & ball glory, breaking down the fabricated myths

of white major league legends, of who was better than who
beating them at their own crap game, with killer bats,
as bud powell swung his silence into beauty of a josh
gibson home run, skittering across piano keys of bleachers
shattering all manufactured legends up there in lights
struck out white knights, on the risky edge of amazement
awe, the miraculous truth sluicing through
steeped & disguised in the blues
confluencing, like the point at the cross
when a fastball hides itself up in a slider, curve
breaking down & away in a wicked, sly grin
curved & posed as an ass-scratching uncle tom, who
like old sachel paige delivering his famed hesitation pitch
before coming back with a hard, high, fast one, is slicker
sliding, & quicker than a professional hitman—
the deadliness of it all, the sudden strike
like that of the "brown bomber's" crossing right
of sugar ray robinson's, lightning, cobra bite

& you, there, father, through it all, catching rhythms of chono
pozo balls, drumming, like conga beats into your catcher's
    mitt
hard & fast as "cool papa" bell jumping into bed
before the lights went out

of the old, negro baseball league, a promise, you were
father, a harbinger, of shock waves, soon come

BOOMERANG: A BLATANTLY POLITICAL POEM

eye use to write poems about burning
down the motherfucking country for crazy
horse, geronimo & malcolm king
x, use to (w)rite about stabbing white folks
in their air-conditioned eyeballs with ice picks
cracking their sagging balls with sledgehammer blows
now, poems leap from the snake-tip of my tongue
bluesing a language twisted tighter than braided hope
hanging like a limp-noosed rope down the question mark
back of some coal miner's squaw, her razor slanted
killer shark eyes swollen shut with taboos
she thought she heard & knew
the sun in a voice looking like bessie smith's severed arm
on that mississippi back road, screaming, like a dead man's
        son
who had to watch his old man eat his own pleading heart
& sometimes eye wonder if it's worth the bother
of it all, these poems eye (w)rite holding
language percolating & shaped
into metaphoric rage
underneath, say
a gentle simile, like a warm
spring day, soft as balm or talcum
on the edge of a tornado that hits quicker
than the flick of a bat's wing nicking the eye

eye use to write poems about killing fools like ronald reagan
daffy duck grinning off 30 million sucked down
the whirlpooling black holes of cia space
director casey taking a lobotomy
hit, slash to protect
the gipper
dumb
motherfuckers
everywhere tying bombs
to their own tongues, lighting fuses

of staged events that lye of peace & saving
money in the s & l pirateering, like president gipper
they are metaphors for all that's wrong in america right now
all this cloning, brouhaha, paid mouthpieces on wall street
& the gipper giving frying skillet speeches, that ray gun reagan
ray gunning america, now, cannibalizing airwaves
with mouthpieces fronting slimy churches
building up humongous bank accounts
in the name of the holy bones
of jesus christ, long gone
& dead
& it is a metaphor
boomeranging jimmy
& tammy bakker, sleazy swaggert
vacuuming pocketbooks of the old & the dead
like medusa meese heads nicked off & sluicing like bad faith
they dangle heads from "freedom fighter" mouths
tell the black bird press herded up on a wire
that it's okay, it's okay,
it's okay

eye use to write poems about burning
down the motherfucking country for crazy
horse, geronimo & malcolm king
x marks the spot where "coons" signed away
their lives on dotted lines, black holes
sucking away their breath
for a sack of cotton
full of woe & so
eye
sit here
now, (w)riting
poems of the soft
calm beauty welling
in my son's innocent 4 year
old eyes, thinking, perhaps of the time

when this rage will strike him, driving him towards madness
knowing all the while it will come quicker than quick
sooner than expected
& nothing
absolutely nothing
will have been undone

AMY UYEMATSU

FORTUNE COOKIE BLUES

i

The way I hear it, Chinese fortune cookies
are about as authentic
as Hollywood's Charlie Chan,
only this story has a better twist
(not slant) to it.
They were concocted by some shrewd issei
who came over on a Japanese freighter.
He probably borrowed the idea—
the Chinese I know say any invention
can be traced back to the Middle Kingdom,
and everyone knows that Japanese
are called great imitators.
So this issei's son opens a little bakery
after their release
from that barbed wire camp.
They made an instant fortune conning
Americans whose idea of real Chinese food
is chop suey—and dessert,
a piece of Confucian wisdom
ingeniously packaged in one small,
mysterious cookie.

ii

My father's father named his third son Star,
just like he named the nursery
which made him rich during the Thirties.
Some say Grandpa's old hands were magical,
breeding lush red camellias and pink azaleas
for species and shadings not yet named.
Stiff branches of juniper bent with ease
wherever his hands led them.
But Star died before turning sixteen,
and all of Grandpa's land, flowers,
secrets he discovered in the soil

and carefully recorded in diaries
were left to the remaining children—
whose hands were never magical.

iii

I wonder if gambling is passed on
in the blood, especially for Japanese.
What other little country would dare
attack at Pearl Harbor? What forces
an American minority, falsely imprisoned
as traitors, to enlist in the Army,
calling ourselves "Go for Broke"—
this nisei counterpart to kamikaze?
Can a defeated people,
bombed at Hiroshima and Nagasaki,
recover in just one generation?
In the fifth grade Barney Barnes,
whose mother was half Cherokee,
asked me about World War II movies,
"Which side do you cheer for?"
I was sure he'd betrayed me.
Ten years later he died in 'Nam.

iv

Before I didn't take fortune-telling seriously,
didn't know my ancestors tied paper wishes onto trees,
thin ribbons catching the wind,
whispering messages to the dead,
the living confident that even these tiny paper flags
would not go unnoticed by the gods.

v

There's a nisei woman three blocks away.
Her husband gambled in the big time,
died suddenly when he couldn't pay up.
Now she lives in her grey Mercedes Benz,

her home cluttered with clothing and newspapers.
She parks on the land he left her,
land worth millions now,
where she eats and sleeps,
refusing to leave her car,
always keeping one eye on her rearview mirror.

vi

My son grows up in a different time.
He can't be singled out like I was,
the only Japanese in a small WASP town.
Too many of us now to bully anymore.
I should be happy for him.
But just last week two kids on bikes
circled me with "Ching Chong" insults,
and nothing I said could make them see me.

DECEMBER 7 ALWAYS BRINGS CHRISTMAS EARLY

All persons of Japanese ancestry, both alien
and nonalien, will be evacuated from the above
designated area by 12:00 noon.

    —Executive Order 9066, Franklin D. Roosevelt, 1942

december 7 always brings christmas early
in neat white packages
red circles perfectly centered
one to a side

mama was taken away in a long railed box
blinds pulled taut to hold in her shame

they delivered her to a box in santa anita
walls lined with tissue paper hay
layered over manure and the bloody vomit
that gushes from caged animals

they confined her to a tarbacked box
in that flattened arizona desert
and in aerial photographs
the human cartons arranged row by row
framed by impeccably straight cornered wire borders
were picture perfect

they put me in an airless box
every december 7
when the history lesson was me
they gave me to babies
who were just learning the habits
of their fathers

forty years later the presents arrive
in one continuing commemoration
each precisely wrapped in black and white newsprint
houston st. louis new york
davis boston west philadelphia

in detroit the autoworker at the bar
didn't need to know the skull he smashed
belonged to vincent chin a name that didn't match

the evacuation of bodies resumes
judged by the same eyes that watched mama's train

Ellen Bryant Voigt

AT THE MOVIE: VIRGINIA, 1956

This is how it was:
they had their own churches, their own schools,
schoolbuses, football teams, bands and majorettes,
separate restaurants, in all the public places
their own bathrooms, at the doctor's
their own waiting room, in the *Tribune*
a column for their news, in the village
a neighborhood called Sugar Hill,
uneven rows of unresponsive houses
that took the maids back in each afternoon—
in our homes used the designated door,
on Trailways sat in the back, and at the movie
paid at a separate entrance, stayed upstairs.
Saturdays, a double feature drew the local kids
as the town bulged, families surfacing
for groceries, medicine and wine,
the black barber, white clerks in the stores—crowds
lined the sidewalks, swirled through the courthouse yard,
around the stone soldier and the flag,

and still I never *saw* them on the street.
It seemed a chivalric code
laced the milk: you'd try not to look
and they would try to be invisible.
Once, on my way to the creek,
I went without permission to the tenants'
log cabin near the barns, and when Aunt Susie
opened the door, a cave yawned, and beyond her square,
leonine, freckled face, in the hushed interior,
Joe White lumbered up from the table, six unfolding
feet of him, dark as a gun-barrel, his head bent
to clear the chinked rafters, and I caught
the terrifying smell of sweat and grease,
smell of the woodstove, nightjar, straw mattress—

This was rural Piedmont, upper south;
we lived on a farm but not in poverty.

When finally we got our own TV, the evening news
with its hooded figures of the Ku Klux Klan
seemed like another movie—*King Solomon's Mines,*
the serial of Atlantis in the sea.
By then I was thirteen,
and no longer went to movies to see movies.
The downstairs forged its attentions forward,
toward the lit horizon, but leaning a little
to one side or the other, arranging the pairs
that would own the county, stores and farms, everything
but easy passage out of there—
and through my wing-tipped glasses the balcony
took on a sullen glamor: whenever the film
sputtered on the reel, when the music died
and the lights came on, I swiveled my face
up to where they whooped and swore,
to the smoky blue haze and that tribe
of black and brown, licorice, coffee,
taffy, red oak, sweet tea—

wanting to look, not knowing how to see,
I thought it was a special privilege
to enter the side door, climb the stairs
and scan the even rows below—trained bears
in a pit, herded by the stringent rule,
while they were free, lounging above us,
their laughter pelting down on us like trash.

MARILYN NELSON WANIEK

WOMEN'S LOCKER ROOM

The splat of bare feet on wet tile
breaks the incredible luck
of my being alone in here.
I snatch a stingy towel
and sidle into the shower. I'm already soaped
by the time a white hand turns the neighboring knob.
I recognize the arm as one that flashed
for many rapid laps while I dogpaddled at the shallow end.
I dart an appraising glance: She arches down
to wash her lifted heel, and is beautiful.
As she straightens, I look into her eyes.

For an instant I remember human sacrifice:
The female explorer led skyward,
her blond tresses loose on her neck;
the drums of our pulses grew louder;
I raised the obsidian knife.
Violets bloomed in the clefts of the stairs.

I could freeze her name in an ice cube,
bottle the dirt from her footsteps
with potent graveyard dust.
I could gather the combings from her hairbrush
to burn with her fingernail clippings,
I could feed her Iago powder.
Childhood taunts, branded ears,
a thousand insults swirl through my memory
like headlines in a city vacant lot.

I jump, grimace, divide like an amoeba
into twin rages that stomp around
with their lips stuck out,
then come suddenly face to face.
They see each other and know that they
are mean mamas.
Then I bust out laughing
and let the woman live.

STAR-FIX

For Melvin M. Nelson, Captain USAF (ret.)
(1917–1966)

At his cramped desk
under the astrodome,
the navigator looks
thousands of light-years
everywhere but down.
He gets a celestial fix,
measuring head-winds;
checking the log;
plotting wind-speed,
altitude, drift
in a circle of protractors,
slide-rules, and pencils.

He charts in his Howgozit
the points of no alternate
and of no return.
He keeps his eyes on the compass,
the two altimeters, the map.
He thinks, *Do we have enough fuel?*
What if my radio fails?

He's the only Negro in the crew.
The only black flyer on the whole base,
for that matter. Not that it does:
this crew is a team.
Bob and Al, Les, Smitty, Nelson.

Smitty, who said once
after a poker game,
I love you, Nelson.
I never thought I could love
a colored man.
When we get out of this man's Air Force,
if you ever come down to Tuscaloosa,

look me up and come to dinner.
You can come in the front door, too;
hell, you can stay overnight!
Of course, as soon as you leave,
I'll have to burn down my house.
Because if I don't
my neighbors will.

The navigator knows where he is
because he knows where he's been
and where he's going.
At night, since he can't fly
by dead-reckoning,
he calculates his position
by shooting a star.

The octant tells him
the angle of a fixed star
over the artificial horizon.
His position in that angle
is absolute and true:
Where the hell are we, Nelson?
Alioth, in the Big Dipper.
Regulus. Antares, in Scorpio.

He plots their lines
of position on the chart,
gets his radio bearing,
corrects for lost time.

Bob, Al, Les, and Smitty
are counting on their navigator.
If he sleeps,
they all sleep.
If he fails
they fall.

The navigator keeps watch
over the night and the instruments,
going hungry for five or six hours
to give his flight-lunch
to his two little girls.

ALDERMAN

One year the town Republicans
asked Pomp if he would mind
if they put him up for office.
Pomp told them they were kind,
but he had seven children
and a wife he cared about:
He was too young to die—
which he sure would, without a doubt,
if his name stood on that ballot.
Two white men came to call
a few days later at his store,
younger than he, but tall
like he was. They told Pomp he was their brother:
It ain't your fault you had a nigra mother.
They said they'd stand behind him if he ran.

After they left, the local Ku Klux Klan
sent Pomp a message: *Boy, we understand
you need to learn your place.* And Pomp withdrew
because the Klan was wrong: By God, he knew.

TOM WAYMAN

HATING JEWS

How much work
it must be to despise the Jews.
Fourteen million people, or more:
a majority of whom you've never met
but every one
has to be hated. Anti-Semites surely deserve some credit
for undertaking this collosal task.

And speaking of Semites, what about women and men
who hate Arabs? There are more Arabs
than Jews: some who dwell in the desert
and can't read or write,
some who ride around in air-conditioned limousines
rich as Jews are supposed to be.
What an effort is required
to detest so many social groups:
urban, nomads, electronic
specialists, nurses, irrigation technicians.

Meantime, certain individuals
loathe Orientals. I think these haters
should receive an international prize
for their willingness to abhor such a high percentage
of their own species. But others
hate homosexuals
or lesbians, or all men
or women—the latter two projects
being probably the largest ever initiated
in human history.

Yet having an aversion
only to Jews
is such a mammoth endeavor
no wonder those who tackle it
look drained: faces twisted, body slumped.
A few pros after years of training
carry it off more comfortably.

But ordinary women and men who sign up for this activity
seem to my eyes heavily burdened.

And me? I am repulsed
by those human beings who do me harm.
I'm not as ambitious as
the big-league despisers, though.
I attempt to focus my disgust
on specific individuals
causing pain to myself or my friends.
It's true I've learned to dislike
some general classifications of people
—for example, landlords and employers.
But rather than loathe each one of them
I try to remember the source of their odiousness
is the structure that gives them
their power over me
and aim my rage at that.

So I'm not against hate. I consider some of it
excellent for the circulation: enough injustice
remains on this planet
to justify hate being with us a while yet.
My intent is
to see it directed
where it will do the most good.

MICHAEL S. WEAVER

THE PICNIC, AN HOMAGE TO CIVIL RIGHTS

We spread torn quilts and blankets,
mashing the grass under us until it was hard,
piled the baskets of steamed crabs
by the trees in columns that hid the trunk,
put our water coolers of soda pop
on the edges to mark the encampment,
like gypsies settling in for revelry
in a forest in Rumania or pioneers
blazing through the land of the Sioux,
the Apache, and the Arapaho, looking guardedly
over our perimeters for poachers
or the curious noses of fat women
ambling past on the backs of their shoes.
The sun crashed through the trees,
tumbling down and splattering in shadows
on the baseball diamond like mashed bananas.
We hunted for wild animals in the clumps
of forests, fried hot dogs until the odor
turned solid in our nostrils like wood.
We were in the park.

One uncle talked incessantly, because he knew
the universe; another was the griot
who stomped his foot in syncopation
to call the details from the base of his mind;
another was a cynic who doubted everything,
toasting everyone around with gin.
The patriarchal council mumbled on,
while the women took the evening to tune
their hearts to the slow air and buzzing flies,
to hold their hands out so angels could stand
in their palms and give dispensation,
as we played a rough game of softball
in the diamond with borrowed gloves,
singing Chuck Berry and Chubby Checker,
diving in long lines into the public pool,

throwing empty peanut shells to the lion,
buying cotton candy in the aviary
of the old mansion, laughing at monkeys,
running open-mouthed and full in the heat
until our smell was pungent and natural,
while the sun made our fathers and uncles
fall down in naps on their wives' laps, and
we frolicked like wealthy children on an English estate,
as reluctant laws and bloodied heads
tacked God's theses on wooden doors,
guaranteed the canopy of the firmament above us.

C. K. WILLIAMS

RACISTS

Vas en Afrique! Back to Africa! the butcher we used to
    patronize in the rue Cadet market,
beside himself, shrieked at a black man in an argument the
    rest of the import of which I missed
but that made me anyway for three years walk an extra
    street to a shop of definitely lower quality
until I convinced myself that probably I'd misunderstood
    that other thing and could come back.
Today another black man stopped, asking something that
    again I didn't catch, and the butcher,
who at the moment was unloading his rotisserie, slipping
    the chickens off their heavy spit,
as he answered—how get this right?—casually but accurately
    brandished the still-hot metal,
so the other, whatever he was there for, had subtly to lean
    away a little, so as not to flinch.

ROBERT WINNER

SEGREGATED RAILWAY DINER—1946

I sat down in the colored section
in my sixteen-year-old's gesture.
He sat facing me in his life.

A thin smile licked his lips
and disappeared in the corners. Outside,
gray unpainted cabins, red clay yards
where black men and their calico women
watched the slick trains pass—

It buried me, that smile. It said
I didn't know enough to sit with him
in that lacerated corner.

He studied his plate when the captain came over,
M.P. face the color of butcher's meat—
rapping me on the shoulder with a heavy pencil,
arm grip steering me to my assigned seat.

NELLIE WONG

CAN'T TELL

When World War II was declared
on the morning radio,
we glued our ears, widened our eyes.
Our bodies shivered.

A voice said
Japan was the enemy,
Pearl Harbor a shambles
and in our grocery store
in Berkeley, we were suspended

next to the meat market
where voices hummed,
valises, pots and pans packed,
no more hot dogs, baloney,
pork kidneys.

We children huddled on wooden planks
and my parents whispered:
We are Chinese, we are Chinese.
Safety pins anchored,
our loins ached.

Shortly our Japanese neighbors vanished
and my parents continued to whisper:
We are Chinese, we are Chinese.

We wore black arm bands,
put up a sign
in bold letters.

BARON WORMSER

SOUL MUSIC

The Baltimore evening I saw
Otis and Aretha I knew
Kings and queens existed after all:
Something good and true and danceable,
The uncharted earthbound hit.

They said to believe and leap.
The nation no longer was diagrammatic;
Unsevered feeling fit
Into anybody's skin.
Unthwarted sound was the test
Of embodied, unchurched progress.

Outside that night
Plate glass fractured like
A sobbing final tone,
A plea which brought white men
To the city on a Sunday afternoon
To watch the condemned frolic
At everyone's expense.

Whole blocks burned gladly,
The stuff of democratic
Promise freely redeemed,
The grandeur of performance
Burlesqued by riot.

I, too, protested:
Hadn't I been good,
Hadn't I endorsed
Both sympathy and force?
Didn't I love the music
As much as I could?

On the televised streets
I saw people dancing,
Souls on fire with a passion
That sang of days
No ticket could touch.

JAMES WRIGHT

ON A PHRASE FROM SOUTHERN OHIO

for Etheridge Knight

A long time's gone.
Now all I recall for sure
Is a long shattering of jackhammers that stripped
Away the whole one side of one foothill of one
Appalachian mountain

Across the river from me where I was born.
It is summer chilblain, it is blowtorch, it is not
Maiden and morning on the way up that cliff.
Not where I come from.

It is a slab of concrete that for all I know
Is beginning to crumble.

Once,
Lazy and thieving toward the dark of an afternoon,
Shamba, Dick, Crum, Apie, Beanie, Bernardo,
And I got hold of a skiff,
And crawled all the way over to West Virginia
To the narrow hot mud shore, the foot
Of the scarred mountain.

Then from the bottom
Of that absolutely
Smooth dead
Face
We
Climbed
Straight up
And white

To a garden of bloodroots, tangled there, a vicious secret
Of trilliums, the dark purple silk sliding its hands deep down
In the gorges of those savage flowers, the only
Beauty we found, outraged in that naked hell.

Well, we found two black boys up there
In the wild cliff garden.
Well, we beat the hell out of one
And chased out the other.

And still in my dreams I sway like one fainting strand
Of spiderweb, glittering and vanishing and frail
Above the river.
What were those purple shadows doing
Under the ear
Of the woman who was weeping along the Ohio
River the woman?
Damned if you know;
I don't.

AL YOUNG

A POEM FOR PLAYERS

Yes, theyll let you play,
let you play third base or fender bass,
let you play Harrah's Club or Shea Stadium

Theyll let you play
in a play anyway: Shakespeare,
Ionesco, Bullins, Baraka, or Genet,
only dont get down *too* much
& dont go gettin too uppity

Theyll let you play,
oh yes, on the radio, stereo,
even on the video, Ojays,
O.J. Simpson, only please dont stray
too far from your ghetto rodeo

Theyll let you be Satchmo,
theyll let you be Diz,
theyll let you be Romeo,
     or star in *The Wiz*
but you gots to remember that
     that's all there is

Oh, you can be a lawyer or a medico,
a well-briefcased executive with Texaco;
you can even get yourself hired, man,
to go teach *Ulysses* in Dublin, Ireland

Theyll let you play
so long as you dont play around,
so long as you play it hot or cool,
so long as you dont play down the blues
theyll let you play in *Playboy, Playgirl,*
or the *Amsterdam News*

Finally theyll let you play
politics if you dont get in the way

some of us did and had to be
iced by conspiracy, international mystery

Theyll let you play anybody but you,
that's pretty much what they will do

W. H. AUDEN & MANTAN MORELAND

in memory of the Anglo-American poet & the
Afro-American comic actor (famed for his role
as Birmingham Brown, chauffeur in those ancient
Charlie Chan movies) who died on the same day
in 1973

Consider them both in paradise,
discussing one another—
the one a poet, the other an actor;
interchangeable performers
who finally slipped backstage
of a play whose cast favored lovers.

"You executed some brilliant lines,
Mr. Auden, & doubtless engaged our
innermost emotions & informed imagination,
for I pondered your *Age of Anxiety*
diligently over a juicy order of ribs."

"No shit!" groans Auden, mopping his brow.
"I checked out all your Charlie Chan
flicks & flipped when you turned up again
in *Watermelon Man* & that gas commercial
over TV. Like, where was you all that
time in between? I thought you'd done
died & gone back to England or somethin."

"Wystan, pray tell, why did you ever eliminate
that final line from 'September 1, 1939'?—
We must all love one another or die."

That was easy. We gon die anyway no matter
how much we love, but the best thing I like
that you done was the way you buck them eyes
& make out like you running sked all the time.
Now, that's the bottom line of the black
experience where you be in charge of the scene.
For the same reason you probly stopped shufflin."

K EVIN YOUNG

NO OFFENSE

If you wonder why
I'm not laughing, go ask
Brian, the sixth grade cut-up
the one with the most dirty jokes
who requested the tribal African song
Tina Singu, each music class, black
vinyl spinning while Brian made
faces, knocked his knees together
like eggs. If you are curious about
me, just ask the boy who riddled
the whole playground or me
& my friends walking
home: *What do you get*
when you cross a black person

with a smurf? I am sure today
he would answer you, would explain
now that he meant No offense just
like he did then above the crowd
of girls leaning close or the boys
trying to get his timing down,
just as after the punchline
he always said *You know I don't*
mean you. It's OK. And when
you see that boy whose last name
I don't seem to remember, be sure
to tell him that this here Smigger

could care less yet could never care
more, that my blue
& brown body is more
than willing to inform
him offense is one hostage
I have never taken.

AL ZOLYNAS

LOVE IN THE CLASSROOM

—for my students

Afternoon. Across the garden, in Green Hall,
someone begins playing the old piano—
a spontaneous piece, amateurish and alive,
full of a simple, joyful melody.
The music floats among us in the classroom.

I stand in front of my students
telling them about sentence fragments.
I ask them to find the ten fragments
in the twenty-one-sentence paragraph on page forty-five.
They've come from all parts
of the world—Iran, Micronesia, Africa,
Japan, China, even Los Angeles—and they're still
eager to please me. It's less than half
way through the quarter.

They bend over their books and begin.
Hamid's lips move as he follows
the tortuous labyrinth of English syntax.
Yoshie sits erect, perfect in her pale make-up,
legs crossed, quick pulse minutely
jerking her right foot. Tony,
from an island in the South Pacific, sprawls
limp and relaxed in his desk.

The melody floats around and through us
in the room, broken here and there, fragmented,
re-started. It feels mideastern, but
it could be jazz, or the blues—it could be
anything from anywhere.
I sit down on my desk to wait,
and it hits me from nowhere—a sudden,
sweet, almost painful love for my students.

"Nevermind," I want to cry out.
"It doesn't matter about fragments.

Finding them or not. Everything's
a fragment and everything's not a fragment.
Listen to the music, how fragmented,
how whole, how we can't separate the music
from the sun falling on its knees on all the greenness,
from this moment, how this moment
contains all the fragments of yesterday
and everything we'll ever know of tomorrow!"

Instead, I keep a coward's silence.
The music stops abruptly;
they finish their work,
and we go through the right answers,
which is to say
we separate the fragments from the whole.

CONTRIBUTORS' NOTES

FRANCISCO ALARCÓN is the author of several books of poetry, including *The Earthquake Poems* and *Tattoos* (both Humanizarte Publications), and *Body in Flames/Cuerpo en Llamas* and *Snake Poems* (both Chronicle Books). His awards include a Writer's Fellowship from the California Arts Council, a Danforth Fellowship, and a Fulbright Fellowship. He is currently a professor at the University of California at Santa Cruz. A native of Los Angeles, Alarcón grew up in Mexico and currently resides in San Francisco.

FAREEDAH ALLAH (AKA Ruby Constance Saunders) holds degrees from Hampton University (1961) and Howard University (1987). She is a math teacher in Washington, D.C.

CARROLL ARNETT/GOGISGI, Cherokee. "Born and reared in Oklahoma and the Marine Corps, the old one. Transplanted to west central Michigan in 1970. Most recent book: *Night Perimeter: New and Selected Poems 1958–1990* (Greenfield Review Press, 1991). I make money, spend money, and clean. I write, shoot all manner of small arms, and smoke. I pray to and for the Earth. All the time."

RUSSELL ATKINS began publishing as an experimental writer in the 1940s. *Beloit Poetry Journal, Poetry NOW, Western Review, Gamut,* and a number of anthologies have printed his work. He has received fellowships from the Ohio Arts Council, an honorary doctorate from Cleveland State University, and other awards. He is a composer of music. His books include *Phenomena,* 1961, *Objects,* 1963, *Here in The,* 1976, and *Juxtapositions,* 1991.

JIMMY SANTIAGO BACA, an ex-convict who taught himself to read while in prison, is the author of *Immigrants in Our Own Land & Selected Early Poems, Martin & Meditations on the South Valley,* and *Black Mesa,* all published by New Directions. He received an American Book Award from the Before Columbus Foundation in 1988.

PETER BLUE CLOUD is a Turtle Mohawk from Caughnawaga, Quebec and a former ironworker. He has served as editor of the *Alcatraz Newsletter,* poetry editor of *Akwesasne Notes,* and co-editor of *Coyote's Journal.* He has published six books, including *Elderberry Flute Song* and *White Corn Sister.*

GWENDOLYN BROOKS was born in 1917. She has received two Guggenheim fellowships, a grant from the National Institute of Arts and Letters, and the Pulitzer Prize for *Annie Allen,* her second book of poems. In 1969 Gwendolyn Brooks was named Poet Laureate of the State of Illinois, an honor formerly held by Carl Sandburg.

CHARLES BUKOWSKI was born in Andernach, Germany in 1920, and brought to the United States at the age of two. He was raised in Los Angeles. He is the author of more than twenty books of poetry and prose. He died in 1994.

LORNA DEE CERVANTES is the author of *Emplumada* (University of Pittsburgh Press) and *From the Cables of Genocide* (Arte Publico, 1991).

DARYL NGEE CHINN has been a television cameraman, camera salesman, househusband, Chinese cooking instructor, father, carpenter, admissions counselor, and editor of a literary magazine. His book, *Soft Parts of the Back,* was published by the University of Central Florida Press in 1989.

LUCILLE CLIFTON is the author of eight volumes of poetry, most recently, *The Book of Light,* published in 1993 by Copper Canyon. She is the Distinguished Professor of Humanities at St. Mary's College of Maryland.

SAM CORNISH is founder, with his spouse, Florella Orowan, of the Fiction, Literature & the Arts Bookstore in Brookline, Massachusetts. He teaches at Emerson College in Boston and is the author of *Songs of Jubilee* (Unicorn Press, 1986). His latest book is *Folks Like Me* (Zoland Books).

JAYNE CORTEZ is the author of six books of poetry, including *Coagulations: New and Selected Poems* (Thunder's Mouth Press, 1984). She has received the Before Columbus Foundation American Book Award (1980) and fellowships from the National Endowment for the Arts (NEA) and the New York Creative Artists Public Service Program.

JIM DANIELS is a native of Detroit. His third book of poems, *M-80,* was published by the University of Pittsburgh Press in 1993. *Niagara Falls,* a long poem, was published as a chapbook by Adastra Press in 1994. He wrote the screenplay for *No Pets,* a feature film directed by Tony Buba released in 1994.

Born in Detroit, Michigan, **TOI DERRICOTTE** has published three collections of poetry, *Natural Birth* (Crossing Press), *The Empress of the Death House* (Lotus Press), and most recently *Captivity* (University of Pittsburgh Press), which is in its third printing. Among her many honors and awards, Derricotte is the recipient of two fellowships from the NEA, as well as the recipient of the United Black Artists, USA, Inc., Distinguished Pioneering of the Arts Award. She is Associate Professor in the English department at the University of Pittsburgh.

CHITRA BANERJEE DIVAKARUNI was born in 1956 and is originally from India. She teaches creative writing at Foothills College, California. She has published three books of poems, including *Black Candle* from Calyx Books in 1991.

JIMMIE DURHAM, a Wolf Clan Cherokee, was born in Arkansas. During the 1970s he was a member of the Central Council of the American Indian Movement and was a founder and executive director of the International Indian Treaty Council. A book of collected poems, *Columbus Day,* was published by West End Press in 1982.

CORNELIUS EADY is the author of three books of poems. His second book, *Victims of the Latest Dance Craze,* won the Lamont Prize for Poetry in 1985. His third book, *The Gathering of My Name,* was published by Carnegie Mellon University Press in 1991.

ALFRED ENCARNACION currently teaches as part of the adjunct faculty at Temple University. He hope to go to the Philippines to do post-graduate work at the University of San Carlos. His chapbook *At Winter's End* appeared in 1986 from Limbo Press. His poems have appeared in such periodicals as *Asian American, Cape Rock, Indiana Review, Journal of American Culture, Oklawaha Review, Whiskey Island, Wind,* and in anthologies such as *Anthology of Magazine Verse and Yearbook of American Poetry '83, The Open Boat,* and *Unsettling America.*

MARTÍN ESPADA was born in Brooklyn, New York in 1957. He is the author of four poetry collections: *The Immigrant Iceboy's Bolero* (1982), *Trumpets From the Islands of Their Eviction* (1987), *Rebellion is the Circle of a Lover's Hands* (1990), and, most recently, *City of Coughing and Dead Radiators* (1993). He is also the editor of *Poetry Like Bread: Poets of the Political Imagination* from Curbstone Press (1994). He has been awarded two fellowships from the NEA, a Massachusetts Artists' Fellowship, and the PEN/Revson Foundation Fellowship, as well as the Paterson Poetry Prize, for *Rebellion is the Circle of a Lover's Hands.* A former civil rights and tenant lawyer, Espada currently teaches in the English department at the University of Massachusetts-Amherst.

CALVIN FORBES was born in Newark, New Jersey. He has an MA from Brown University. He is the author of *Blue Monday,* (Wesleyan University Press, 1974). *From the Book of Shine,* (Burning Deck Press, 1978 and

Razorback Press (Wales) 1979). He is Associate Professor of Literature in the Liberal Arts department of the School of the Art Institute of Chicago.

CHARLES FORT was born in New Britain, Connecticut, in 1951. He teaches at Southern Connecticut State University. His books include *The Town Clock Burning,* reprinted as a Carnegie Mellon Classic Contemporary, and *Darvil,* a prose-poem sequence (St. Andrew's Press).

CHRISTOPHER GILBERT'S first book of poems, *Across the Mutual Landscape,* was a Walt Whitman Award winner, and he was the 1986 Robert Frost Place resident poet. Among other awards, he has received two NEA poetry fellowships. His new book is called *Demos/Music of the Striving That Was There.* He plays the saxophone and accordion, and lives in Providence, Rhode Island.

DIANE GLANCY teaches Native American Literature and Creative Writing at Macalester College in St. Paul, Minnesota. Her fourth book of poetry, *Lone Dog's Winter Count,* was published by West End Press in 1990. She won the 1990 Native American Prose Award from the University of Nebraska Press for *Claiming Breath,* a collection of essays. The book also won a 1993 American Book Award from the Before Columbus Foundation. She has also written three collections of short stories. The third, *Monkey Secret,* is forthcoming from Triquarterly Books in 1995.

JOY HARJO is an enrolled member of the Muscogee Tribe and lives in Albuquerque, New Mexico. Forthcoming is a new collection of poetry, *The Woman Who Fell From the Sky* (W. W. Norton); *Reinventing the Enemy's Language,* an anthology of native women's writing forthcoming from the University of Arizona Press; and *The Goodluck Cat,* a children's book from Harcourt Brace. She also performs her poetry and plays saxophone with her band, Poetic Justice.

MICHAEL S. HARPER is University Professor and Professor of English at Brown University, where he has taught since 1970. He is the first poet laureate of the State of Rhode Island, a term he held from 1988 to 1993. He has published ten books of poetry. *Images of Kin: New & Selected Poems* won the Melville-Cane Award from the Poetry Society of America; *History is Your Own Heartbeat* won the Black Academy of Arts & Letters Award for Poetry. He has edited the *Collected Poems* of Sterling Brown, which he selected for the National Poetry Series, 1979. He is co-editor of *Every Shut Eye Ain't Asleep,* an anthology of poetry by African Americans since 1945 to the present. *Honorable Amendments* is his latest collection of his poetry, published in 1994. His *Collected Poems* will be published in 1996.

LINDA HOGAN is a Chickasaw poet, novelist, and essayist. She is the author of several books of poetry and a collection of short fiction. Her novel, *Mean Spirit,* published by Atheneum, received the Oklahoma Book Award for fiction, 1990, and the Mountains and Plains Booksellers Award. Her book, *Seeing Through the Sun,* received an American Book Award from the Before Columbus Foundation. *The Book of Medicines,* from Coffee House Press, 1993, has received much critical attention. Hogan is the recipient of an NEA grant, a Guggenheim fellowship, The Five Civilized Tribes Museum Playwriting Award, and many others. She is a professor at the University of Colorado.

GARRETT KAORU HONGO teaches creative writing at the University of Oregon. He is the editor of *The Open Boat: Poems from Asian America,* Anchor Books, 1993.

LANGSTON HUGHES was born in Joplin, Missouri, in 1902. From 1926 until his death in 1967, Langston Hughes devoted his time to writing and lecturing. He wrote poetry, short stories, autobiography, song lyrics, essays, humor, and plays. *The Panther and the Lash,* his last book of poetry, published in 1967, was reissued by Vintage Classics in 1992.

T. R. HUMMER is the author of numerous books of poetry, including *The 18,000-Ton Olympic Dream,* Morrow, 1990. He directs the writing program at the University of Oregon.

DAVID IGNATOW has published fifteen volumes of poetry and three of prose. His awards include the Bollingen Prize, the Wallace Stevens Fellowship, Robert Frost Silver Medal and others. His most recent book of poems is *Against the Evidence: Selected Poems, 1934–94* (Wesleyan). He is Professor Emeritus, City University of New York.

JUNE JORDAN has published twenty books, most recently *Naming Our Destiny: New and Selected Poetry* and *Technical Difficulties: New Political Essays.* Jordan is currently Professor of Afro-American Studies & Women's Studies at the University of California-Berkeley.

LAWRENCE JOSEPH'S three books of poems include *Before Our Eyes* (1993, published by Farrar, Straus & Giroux), and *Curriculum Vitae* (1988) and *Shouting at No One* (1983), published in the Pitt Poetry Series. His poems, essays, and reviews have appeared in *The Paris Review, The*

Nation, The Village Voice, and *Poetry,* among other magazines, and his poems have appeared in numerous anthologies. A professor of law at St. John's University School of Law, he lives in New York City.

LONNY KANEKO'S book of poems, *Coming Home from Camp,* portrays life among Japanese Americans during and after World War II. He has received both national and local awards for his poetry, fiction, and plays—including a fellowship from the NEA for poetry. Stories, poems, and essays appear in anthologies such as *An Ear to the Ground, Dissident Voice, Daily Fare,* and *The Big AIIIEEEEE!* Currently, Lonny is the Chair of the Arts and Humanities Division at Highline College, where he also teaches creative writing. He also serves as Chair of the Washington State Arts Commission.

RICHARD KATROVAS teaches in the MFA Program at the University of New Orleans. A former Fulbright fellow, he is faculty director for the Central European University Summer Writers' Workshop in Prague, Czech Republic. He has published four books, most recently, *The Book of Complaints,* Carnegie Mellon University Press. His stories, poems, reviews, and essays have appeared widely.

CAROLYN KIZER won the Pulitzer Prize in Poetry for *Yin* (BOA Editions) in 1985. Other books of poetry include *The Ungrateful Garden, Mermaids in the Basement, Midnight Was My Cry, Knock Upon Silence,* and *Nearness of You.* She is the founding editor of *Poetry Northwest,* and has won the Roethke Prize and the Robert Frost Medal.

ETHERIDGE KNIGHT was born in Mississippi in 1931. He published four collections of his poems, including *The Essential Etheridge Knight* (University of Pittsburgh Press, 1986). He received fellowships from both the NEA and the Guggenheim Foundation. His work is widely anthologized. He died in 1991.

YUSEF KOMUNYAKAA'S *Neon Vernacular: New and Selected Poems* (Wesleyan University Press) won the Pulitzer Prize for Poetry in 1994. He teaches in the English department at the University of Indiana.

The late **AUDRE LORDE** was born in New York City to West Indian parents. Lorde's portraits of American inner-city life are central to her vision of pain and struggle. *Undersong: Chosen Poems Old and New* was published by W. W. Norton and Co. in 1992.

COLLEEN J. MCELROY lives in Seattle, Washington. McElroy has published collections of poetry and short stories, and writes for stage and television.

Her two latest publications are *Driving Under the Cardboard Pines* (fiction), and *What Madness Brought Me Here: New and Selected Poems, 1968–88.* Winner of the Before Columbus Foundation's American Book Award, she has also received two Fulbright fellowships, two NEA grants, and a Rockefeller Fellowship.

NAOMI LONG MADGETT is author of eight volumes of poetry, covering a span of fifty-two years. These include *Exits and Entrances, Octavia and Other Poems,* and *Remembrances of Spring: Collected Early Poems.* Her work has appeared in more than one hundred anthologies in this country and abroad, and in numerous journals. Among her honors are a 1993 American Book Award and the 1993 Michigan Artist Award. She is professor emerita at Eastern Michigan University, director of Lotus Press, Inc., and senior editor of the Lotus Poetry Series of Michigan State University Press.

THYLIAS MOSS has published five volumes of poetry, including *Rainbow Remnants in Rock Bottom Ghetto Sky,* which was selected by Charles Simic for the National Poetry Series, and *Small Congregations,* a volume of new and selected poems published by Ecco.

DAVID MURA is a poet, creative nonfiction writer, critic, playwright, and performance artist. A *Sansei,* or third-generation Japanese American, Mura is the author of *Turning Japanese: Memoirs of a Sansei* (Anchor Doubleday) which won a 1991 Josephine Miles Book Award from Oakland PEN. His book of poetry, *After We Lost Our Way* (E.P. Dutton) won the 1989 National Poetry Series Contest, and his second book of poetry, *The Colors of Desire,* was published in January 1995 (Anchor Doubleday). He has also written *A Male Grief: Notes on Pornography and Addiction* (Milkweed Editions). He is now currently working on an autobiographical work on race from an Asian-American perspective which will be published by Anchor Doubleday.

SHARON OLDS is the author of four collections of poetry, *Satan Says, The Dead and the Living, The Gold Cell,* and *The Father.* She has received the San Francisco Poetry Center Award, the Lamont Poetry Prize, and the National Book Critics Circle Award. She teaches in the creative writing program at New York University.

SIMON J. ORTIZ, poet, short fiction and non-fiction writer, editor, and storyteller, is author of *Woven Stone, Fightin': New & Collected Stories, From Sand Creek, The People Shall Continue* and other books. In 1992 he wrote the narrative for "Surviving Columbus," a documentary about the Pueblo people of the Southwest. Broadcast by PBS, it is about continued resistance by Pueblos against complete Euro-American domination for five hundred years. Ortiz's newest book is *After and Before the Lightning,* University of Arizona Press, 1994. He has three children, Raho, Rainy, and Sara who are all beautiful.

DUDLEY RANDALL has edited the anthologies *Black Poetry* and *The Black Poets,* and has published poetry in *Poem Counterpoem, Cities Burning, More to Remember, Love You, After the Killing,* and *A Litany of Friends.*

DAVID RAY'S most recent books are *Wool Highways,* (Helicon 9), *Not Far from the River* (Copper Canyon, 1990) and *The Mahararu's New Wall* (Wesleyan University Press, 1989). *Sam's Book,* (also Wesleyan) won the Maurice English Poetry Award for 1988. Ray has published fiction, essays, and poetry in many journals, and has been a recipient of an NEA fellowship for his fiction. He is a professor of English at the University of Missouri-Kansas City.

JOHN REPP is the author of *Thirst Like This* (University of Missouri Press, 1990) and the editor of *How We Live Now* (Bedford Books, 1992). He lives in Edinboro, Pennsylvania.

LEO ROMERO has published three books of poetry: *Agua Negra, Celso,* and *Going Home Away Indian.* His first book of stories, *Rita and Los Angeles,* will be published by the Bilingual Review Press this summer. He has a bookstore in Santa Fe, New Mexico called Books and More Books.

KATE RUSHIN is a feminist poet and teacher with a background in theater and independent radio. She teaches writing workshops for adults and children, and her work has been published in journals and in the anthologies *This Bridge Called My Back* and *An Ear to the Ground.* Her book, *The Black Back-Ups* was published by Firebrand Books in 1993.

IRA SADOFF was born in Brooklyn in 1945. He worked for SNCC (Student Non-violent Coordinating Committee) in 1964. His most recent collection is *The Ira Sadoff Reader;* his *New and Selected Poems* will be published by David Godine.

BETSY SHOLL grew up in Brick Town, New Jersey. Her books include *Changing Faces, Appalachian Winter, Rooms Overhead,* and *The Red Line* (University of Pittsburgh Press), which won the 1991 Associated Writing Programs' award series in poetry. She lives with her family in Portland, Maine and teaches at the University of Southern Maine.

GARY SOTO was born and raised in Fresno, California and now lives in Berkeley. He has written for adults and young adults. His books include *Living Up the Street, Who Will Know Us?, Jesse,* and *Local News,* among ten others. His film "The Pool Party" received the Andrew Carnegie Medal from the American Library Association.

ERNESTO TREJO studied in the writing program at Fresno State University and also spent time studying poetry in Mexico. His first book, *Entering a Life,* was published by Arte Publico Press in 1990. He died in 1991.

GAIL TREMBLAY is author of *Indian Singing in 20th Century America,* Calyx Books, 1990. Her work has also appeared in *A Nation Within, Harper's Anthology of 20th Century Native American Poetry,* and in translation in France of *A Nation Within.*

QUINCY TROUPE is the author of nine books, including four volumes of poetry, the latest of which is *Weather Report: New and Selected Poems* (Harlem River Press, 1991). He is also editor of *James Baldwin: The Legacy* (Touchstone, 1989) and co-author of *Miles: The Autobiography* (Simon & Schuster). Mr. Troupe is the recipient of two American Book Awards. In the winter of 1995, Random House will publish *Artists on the Cutting Edge,* a collection of personal essays on well-known and innovative artists. Troupe's fifth volume of poems, *Avalanche,* will also be published in 1995. He is a professor of Creative Writing and American and Caribbean Literature at the University of California, San Diego and lives in La Jolla, California, with his wife, Margaret, and their son, Porter.

AMY UYEMATSU'S first book, *30 Miles from J-Town,* won the 1992 Nicholas Roerich Poetry Prize and was published by Story Line Press. She is a third-generation Californian of Japanese ancestry and lives in Los Angeles. She is a member of PAAWW (Pacific Asian American Women Writers).

ELLEN BRYANT VOIGT has published four volumes of poetry—*Claiming Kin* (1976), *The Forces of Plenty* (1983), *The Lotus Flowers* (1987), and *Two Trees* (1992). Voigt's widely-anthologized poems have appeared in *The New Yorker, The Atlantic, The New Republic,* and *The Nation* as well as numerous literary journals. A recipient of grants from the NEA and Guggenheim Foundation, she was a 1993 Lila Wallace Visiting Fellow. Voigt, who lives in Cabot, Vermont, is married and has two children.

MARILYN NELSON WANIEK is the author of five books of poetry, *For the Body* (1978), *Mama's Promises* (1985), *The Homeplace* (1990), *Partial*

Truth (1992) and *Magnificat* (1994), and two collections of verse for children. Her honors include a Kent fellowship, a travel grant (for translation) from the Cultural Ministry of Denmark, two creative writing fellowships from the National Endowment for the Arts, and the 1990 Connecticut Arts Award. Married and the mother of a fourteen-year-old son and an eight-year-old daughter, she is a professor of English at the University of Connecticut, Storrs.

TOM WAYMAN has published eleven books of poetry, including *Did I Miss Anything? Selected Poems, 1973–93* (Harbour Publishing). He has also published two books of essays and edited five anthologies of poetry. He lives in Winlaw, British Columbia.

MICHAEL S. WEAVER is a poet and playwright. After spending twelve years working as a warehouseman and journalist in Baltimore, his hometown, Weaver received an NEA fellowship in 1985, the year he entered the graduate writing program at Brown. He has published four books of poetry, *Water Song* (1985), *My Father's Geography* (1992), *Stations in a Dream* (1993), and *Timber and Prayer/the Indian Pond Poems.* He has had two plays produced professionally, *Rosa* and *Elvira and the Lost Prince.* He teaches at Rutgers University in Camden and lives in Philadelphia.

C. K. WILLIAMS' most recent book is *A Dream of Mind,* (Farrar, Straus and Giroux, 1992). He has published many other books of poetry, including *Flesh and Blood,* which won the National Book Critics Circle award in 1988.

The late **ROBERT WINNER'S** complete poems, *The Sanity of Earth and Grass,* was published by Tilbury House in 1994.

NELLIE WONG is the author of two collections of poetry, *Dreams in Harrison Railroad Park* (Kelsey Street Press, 1974) and *The Death of Long Steam Lady* (West End Press, 1986). Active in Radical Women and the Freedom Socialist Party, two socialist feminist organizations, Wong has been a keynote speaker at many conferences on women, Asian Pacific Americans and other people of color, and community activism. Her most recent work has appeared in *The Forbidden Stitch, Making Waves, Dissident Song, The Open Boat* and *No More Masks!* Wong works as an affirmative action analyst at the University of California, San Francisco, and is active in University Professional and Technical Employees.

BARON WORMSER is the author of three books of poetry.

JAMES WRIGHT published twelve books of poetry during his long and distinguished career. His *Above the River: the Complete Poems* was published in 1990. He died in 1980.

AL YOUNG is the author of numerous books of poetry, fiction, and nonfiction. *Heaven: Collected Poems 1956–1990* was published by Creative Arts in 1992.

KEVIN YOUNG'S first book, *Most Way Home,* was selected for the National Poetry Series by Lucille Clifton and will be published in 1995 by William Morrow. He has held a Stegner Fellowship at Stanford and is currently an MFA student at Brown University. His work has appeared in *The Kenyon Review, Poetry, Callaloo, Agni,* and *Ploughshares,* among other journals. He is a member of the Dark Room writer's collective based in Boston.

AL ZOLYNAS was born in Austria of Lithuanian parents in 1945, and since then has moved twenty-eight times. As various times, he has been a kitchen helper, lifeguard, worker in a felt factory, cab driver, road construction worker, poetry editor, Minnesota Out Loud Traveling Poet, volunteer for the Hunger Project, and Fulbright-Hays Fellow to India. He now teaches writing and literature and is Chair of the Department of Liberal and Interdisciplinary Studies at United States International University, San Diego, and resides with his wife in Escondido. His first collection, *New Physics,* was published by Wesleyan University Press. With Fred Moramarco, he is co-editor of the recently published *Men of Our Time: An Anthology of Male Poetry in Contemporary America,* University of Georgia Press, 1992.

ACKNOWLEDGMENTS

"Letter to America" by Francisco Alarcón reprinted from *Body in Flames* © 1990 by Francisco Alarcón. Reprinted by permission of Chronicle Books.

"Lawd, Dese Colored Chillum" by Fareedah Allah reprinted by permission of the author.

"Powwow" and "Song of the Breed" reprinted from *Night Perimeter: New and Selected Poems 1958–1990* by Carroll Arnett/Gogisgi, Greenfield Review Press, 1991. Reprinted by permission of the author.

"Late Bus (After a Series of Hold-Ups)" from *Whichever* © 1978 by Russell Atkins, printed with support from the Ohio Arts Council and *Free Lance Magazine*. Reprinted by permission of the author.

"So Mexicans Are Taking Jobs from Americans," "There Are Black." Jimmy Santiago Baca: *Immigrants In Our Own Land.* Copyright © 1982 by Jimmy Santiago Baca. Reprinted by permission of New Directions Publishing Corp.

"The Old Man's Lazy," by Peter Blue Cloud/Aroniawenrate, Mohawk Nation at Kahnawake, Quebec. Reprinted by permission of the author.

"The Lovers of the Poor." Gwendolyn Brooks © 1991. From *BLACKS*, Third World Press, 1991. Reprinted by permission of the author.

"the black poets" © 1994 by Charles Bukowski. Reprinted from *Mockingbird Wish Me Luck* with the permission of Black Sparrow Press.

"Poem for the Young White Man Who Asked Me How I, an Intelligent, Well-Read Person Could Believe in the War Between Races" is reprinted from *Emplumada,* by Lorna Dee Cervantes, by permission of the University of Pittsburgh Press. © 1981 by Lorna Dee Cervantes.

"Not Translation, Not Poetry," "Skin Color from the Sun" by Daryl Ngee Chinn reprinted from *Soft Parts of the Back* by permission of the University Press of Florida. Copyright © 1989 by the Board of Regents of the State of Florida.

"in white america" copyright © 1987 by Lucille Clifton. Reprinted from *Next: New Poems,* by Lucille Clifton, with the permission of BOA Editions, Ltd., 92 Park Ave. Brockport, NY 14420.

"Fannie Lou Hamer" by Sam Cornish reprinted by permission of the author.

"Give Me the Red on the Black of the Bullet" by Jayne Cortez © 1994 by Jayne Cortez. Reprinted by permission of the author.

"Time, Temperature" is reprinted from *M-80*, by Jim Daniels, by permission of the University of Pittsburgh Press. © 1993 by Jim Daniels.

"St. Peter Claver," "The Weakness," "Blackbottom," and "The Struggle" are reprinted from *Captivity* by Toi Derricotte, by permission of the University of Pittsburgh Press. © 1989 by Toi Derricotte.

"Yuba City School" © by Chitra Banerjee Divakaruni is reprinted from *Black Candle* by permission of the publisher, CALYX Books (1991).

"Columbus Day" by Jimmie Durham reprinted from *Columbus Day* by permission of West End Press.

"Sherbet," "Thrift," "The Supremes," "Why Do So Few Blacks Study Creative Writing?," and "False Arrest" © 1991 by Cornelius Eady. Reprinted from *The Gathering of My Name,* Carnegie Mellon University Press, by permission of the author.

"Bulosan Listens to a Recording of Robert Johnson" by Alfred Encarnacion reprinted by permission of the author.

"Bully" and "Jorge the Church Janitor Finally Quits" from *Rebellion is the Circle of a Lover's Hands/Rebelion es el giro de manos del amante* by Martín Espada. Curbstone Press. Copyright © 1991 by Martín Espada. Distributed by InBook. Used by permission of the author and Curbstone Press.

"The Poet's Shuffle" © Calvin Forbes from *Blue Monday,* Wesleyan University Press. Reprinted by permission of the author.

"For Martin Luther King" by Charles Fort reprinted from *The Town Clock Burning,* Carnegie Mellon University Press, by permission of the author.

"Pushing" and "Theory of Curve" by Christopher Gilbert reprinted by permission of the author.

"Kemo Sabe" and "The First Reader, Santee Training School, 1873" by Diane Glancy reprinted from *Lone Dog's Winter Count* by permission of the author and West End Press.

"Anchorage" from the book, *She Had Some Horses* by Joy Harjo. Copyright © 1983 by Joy Harjo. Used by permission of the publisher, Thunder's Mouth Press.

Joy Harjo, "Autobiography" from *In Mad Love & War,* copyright 1990 by Joy Harjo by permission of the University Press of New England.

"Song: *I Want a Witness*" is reprinted from *Song: I Want a Witness,* by Michael S. Harper, by permission of the University of Pittsburgh Press. © 1972 by Michael S. Harper.

"The Truth Is" by Linda Hogan from Coffee House Press reprinted by permission of the author.

"Redress: Thinking It Through" by Garrett Kaoru Hongo reprinted by permission of the author.

"Sweet Words on Race," "Dinner Guest: Me" from *The Panther and the Lash* by Langston Hughes. Copyright © 1967 by Arna Bontemps and George Houston Bass. Reprinted by permission of Alfred A. Knopf, Inc.

"The Ideal," © 1987 by T. R. Hummer, reprinted from *Lower-Class Heresy* (University of Illinois Press) by permission of the author and publisher.

David Ignatow's "Harold" from *Ignatow Poems 1934–69* copyright 1979 by David Ignatow; "For Medgar Evers," from *Rescue the Dead,* copyright 1968 by David Ignatow. Wesleyan University Press by permission of University Press of New England.

"A Poem about Intelligence for My Brothers and Sisters" and "What Would I Do White" reprinted from the book, *Naming Our Destiny* by June Jordan, © 1989 by June Jordan. Used by permission of the publisher, Thunder's Mouth Press.

"Sand Nigger" is reprinted from *Curriculum Vitae,* by Lawrence Joseph, by permission of the University of Pittsburgh Press © 1988 by Lawrence Joseph.

"Bailey Gatzert: The First Grade, 1945" from *An Ear to the Ground,* University of Georgia Press, 1989. Copyright © by Lonny Kaneko. Reprinted by permission of the author.

"Black English" and "Sky" by Richard Katrovas reprinted from *The Book of Complaints,* Carnegie Mellon University Press, 1993. By permission of the author.

"Race Relations" by Carolyn Kizer, from *Yin,* BOA Editions, 1984. Reprinted by permission of the author.

"Dark Prophecy: I Sing of Shine," "For Black Poets Who Think of Suicide," "The Warden Said to Me the Other Day," and "A Wasp Woman Visits a Black Junkie in Prison" are reprinted from *The Essential Etheridge Knight,* by Etheridge Knight, by permission of the University of Pittsburgh Press. © 1986 by Etheridge Knight.

"Report from the Skull's Diorama," "Tu Do Street" by Yusef Komunyakaa from *Dien Cai Dau,* Wesleyan University Press, 1988. Reprinted by permission of the author.

"Afterimages" is reprinted from *Undersong, Chosen Poems Old and New,* Revised Edition, by Audre Lorde, by permission of W.W. Norton & Company, Inc. Copyright © 1992, 1982, 1976, 1974, 1973, 1970, 1968 by Audre Lorde.

"Foul Line—1987," "From *Homegrown: An Asian American Anthology of Writers*" by Colleen J. McElroy. By permission of the author. From *What Madness Brought Me Here: New and Selected Poems, 1968–88* (Wesleyan University Press, 1990).

"Images," from *Octavia and Other Poems* by Naomi Long Madgett (Chicago: Third World Press, 1988). By permission of the author. "The Race Question" from *Star by Star* by Naomi Long Madgett (Detroit: Harlo, 1965; Evenill, 1970). By permission of the author.

"Lessons from a Mirror" by Thylias Moss from *Pyramid of Bone,* The University Press of Virginia, 1989. By permission of the author.

"Letters from Poston Relocation Camp (1942–45)" by David Mura from *After We Lost Our Way,* E. P. Dutton. Copyright David Mura, 1989, reprinted by permission of the author.

"On the Subway." From *The Gold Cell* by Sharon Olds. Copyright © 1987 by Sharon Olds. Reprinted by permission of Alfred A. Knopf, Inc.

"Upstate" Permission to reprint granted by author, Simon J. Ortiz. "Upstate" originally appeared in *A Good Journey,* University of Arizona Press, 1992.

"Black Poet, White Critic," and "The Idiot" by Dudley Randall. Reprinted by permission of the author.

"The Eskimo Girl" by David Ray. Copyright by David Ray. Used by permission of the author.

"Going Full-Court" by John Repp. From *Thirst Like This,* University of Missouri Press, 1990. Reprinted by permission of the author.

"If Marilyn Monroe" by Leo Romero was originally published in *Going Home Away Indian* (Ahsahta Press, Boise State University). Reprinted by permission of the author.

"The Black Back-Ups" from *The Black Back-Ups* by Kate Rushin © copyright 1993 by Kate Rushin. Firebrand Books, 141 The Commons, Ithaca, New York 14850. Reprinted by permission of the author and publisher.

"Civil Rights" by Ira Sadoff originally appeared in *The Ontario Review.* "Civil Rights" and "Nazis" appeared in *Emotional Traffic,* by Ira Sadoff (David Godine, 1989). Reprinted by permission of the author.

"Midnight Vapor Light Breakdown," "Outside the Depot," and "Dawn" are reprinted from *The Red Line,* by Betsy Sholl, by permission of the University of Pittsburgh Press. © 1992 by Betsy Sholl.

"Mexicans Begin Jogging" by Gary Soto is reprinted from *New and Selected Poems* by Gary Soto, © 1995, published by Chronicle Books. By permission of the author and publisher.

"The Cloud Unfolding" by Ernesto Trejo is reprinted with permission from the publisher of *Entering a Life* (Houston: Arte Publico Press-University of Houston, 1990).

"Indian Singing in 20th Century America" by Gail Tremblay from *Indian Singing in 20th Century America,* (Calyx Press, Corvallis, Oregon 1990). Reprinted by permission of the author.

"Poem for My Father," "Boomerang: A Blatantly Political Poem" © from *Weather Reports: New and Selected Poems,* Harlem Review Press © 1991 by Quincy Troupe. Reprinted by permission of the author.

"Fortune Cookie Blues" and "December 7 Always Brings Christmas Early" reprinted from *30 Miles from J-Town* (Story Line Press, 1992) by Amy Uyematsu. Copyright © 1992 by Amy Uyematsu. Reprinted by permission of the author.

"At the Movie: Virginia, 1956" is reprinted from *The Lotus Flowers,* poems by Ellen Bryant Voigt, by permission of the author and W.W. Norton & Company, Inc. Copyright © 1987 by Ellen Bryant Voigt.

"Women's Locker Room" from *Mama's Promises,* by Marilyn Nelson Waniek. Copyright © 1985 by the author, published by Louisiana State University Press. Used with permission. "Star-Fix" and "Alderman" from *The Homeplace* by Marilyn Nelson Waniek. Copyright © 1990 by the author, published by Louisiana State University Press. Used with permission.

"Hating Jews" by Tom Wayman. Reprinted by permission of the author and Harbour Publishing Co. Ltd.

"The Picnic, an Homage to Civil Rights" by Michael S. Weaver was first published in *Callaloo* magazine and then in *My Father's Geography,* University of Pittsburgh Press, 1993. Reprinted by permission of the author.

"Racists" from *Flesh and Blood* by C. K. Williams. Copyright © 1987 by C. K. Williams. Reprinted by permission of Farrar, Straus & Giroux, Inc.

"Segregated Railway Diner, 1946" is reprinted from *The Sanity of Earth and Grass* by Robert Winner, (Tilbury House, 1994). Reprinted by permission of the publisher.

"Can't Tell" by Nellie Wong. Reprinted by permission of the author.

"Soul Music" by Baron Wormser © copyright by Baron Wormser. Reprinted with the permission of the author.

"On a Phrase from Southern Ohio" from *To A Blossoming Pear Tree* by James Wright. Copyright © 1977 by James Wright. Reprinted by permission of Farrar, Straus & Giroux, Inc.

"A Poem for Players" and "W. H. Auden & Mantan Moreland" © 1976 by Al Young. Reprinted with permission of the author.

"No Offense" by Kevin Young reprinted by permission of the author.

"Love in the Classroom" by Al Zolynas reprinted by permission of the author. © by Al Zolynas. Poem first published in *Gorilla Extract,* No. 1, Gorilla Press, San Diego, CA, 1981.

SUBJECT INDEX

Assimilation:

Civil Rights, Civil Unrest:

Class and Economic Issues:

Education:

Family:

Fantasy and Myth:

History:

Humor, Satire:

Language:

Popular Culture:

Race and the Writer:

Religion:

Segregation:

Solidarity and Survival: